Pastor Nelson
I'm grateful for the opportunity
that your interim here at St
Luke's gives me to learn
to know your
personality - + Hazel's.
Louise Ambuel

Letters Via Chinook

AF544668

Letters Via Chinook:
Life in Montana in the 20's and 30's

by
J. Philip Ambuel
and Louise Ambuel

© 1996 by J. Philip Ambuel
and Louise Ambuel

First Edition

Library of Congress Catalog Card Number: 96-96554

International Standard Book Number 0-9652972-0-9

All rights reserved. No part of this book may be reproduced in any form or by any means, electronic or mechanical, including photocopying, recording, or by any information storage or retrieval system without written permission from the authors.

Printed by The Caxton Printers, Ltd.
Caldwell, Idaho 83605

Dedication

To our parents, among the last of the homesteaders, who met the challenges of the prairie with grace and grit, who survived the double whammy of drought and depression and who made a home we remember with love and gratitude; and to our teachers who added a measure of culture and beauty to our lives.

Contents

Preface

Homesteaders were no doubt lured to Montana for many reasons. Some came in hopes of finding a new and better life, some perhaps to leave behind baggage which they had outgrown. The picture the railroad magnates painted of the West led some to dream of a land of milk and honey. It was far from that. There was blistering heat and bone chilling cold; there were buildings to be built and land to be broken in a new and unfamiliar setting. There was drought and depression - a double whammy that ruined many a dream, particularly if one came on the heels of the other. There were rattlesnakes and grasshoppers; there were miles between these newcomers and their friends and families.

Yet in spite of all these rigors, many learned to love this place, and the young to a large extent took for granted what others might view as deprivation, even in those days. As you read Letters Via Chinook you may be tempted to think the writers were wearing rose colored glasses. Yet I think we have not been overly romantic. There was hard work, and tiresome chores; but there was also much to be enjoyed: neighborhood picnics and baseball games, warm homes and sturdy hearts, a community which "hung together".

When one reads some western history one gets the impression that this was a land of cattle rustlers, wars between sheep and cattle men, a place and a people to be exploited by the copper kings and the big landholders. For us, in the south-eastern corner of Montana, these troubles seemed remote or non-existent. Perhaps one reason was that here the holdings were small, the stakes not so large as in other parts of the West, the homesteaders satisfied with their little bit of earth. Perhaps we needed each other, or perhaps some of these struggles had played themselves out before the first decades of the twentieth century.

Whatever the reasons for the relative harmony in our corner of Montana, as we approach the twenty-first century we look back with love, respect and gratitude on the rugged, hard working people who were our mothers and fathers, our neighbors, our teachers, our mentors and our friends.

The primary motivation for Letters Via Chinook was to leave to the senior author's grandchildren a legacy and an understanding of life on a Montana homestead; but as the letters got underway there was also the desire to keep alive for ourselves and any who might be interested those experiences and memories. Like all history it is fragmentary, and in this case primarily personal, but for all that it preserves a bit of Americana - a bit of the West of the early twentieth century. On the threshold of the twenty first century this seems appropriate. In this fast paced, fast changing time it gives a glimpse of a simpler way of life and in some small measure has allowed the authors' souls to catch up with their bodies. Perhaps it can do the same for others.

Acknowledgements

The authors wish to thank:

Jack, Bruce and David Ambuel for technical assistance.

Jack Ambuel for technical assistance, for the drawings of the Ambuel farm and farmstead and for securing the plat of Powder River County and other information relevant to the letter on the land and farming practices.

Marion Storck Ambuel for her support and encouragement throughout the writing of Letters Via Chinook.

Mildred Kramlich Rea for her assistance in the letter on politics and sources of information in Powder River County.

Dikka Moen Rice for her contribution to the information on Norwegian cuisine in the letter on holidays and celebrations.

The County Clerk, Powder River County, for the plat map of Powder River County.

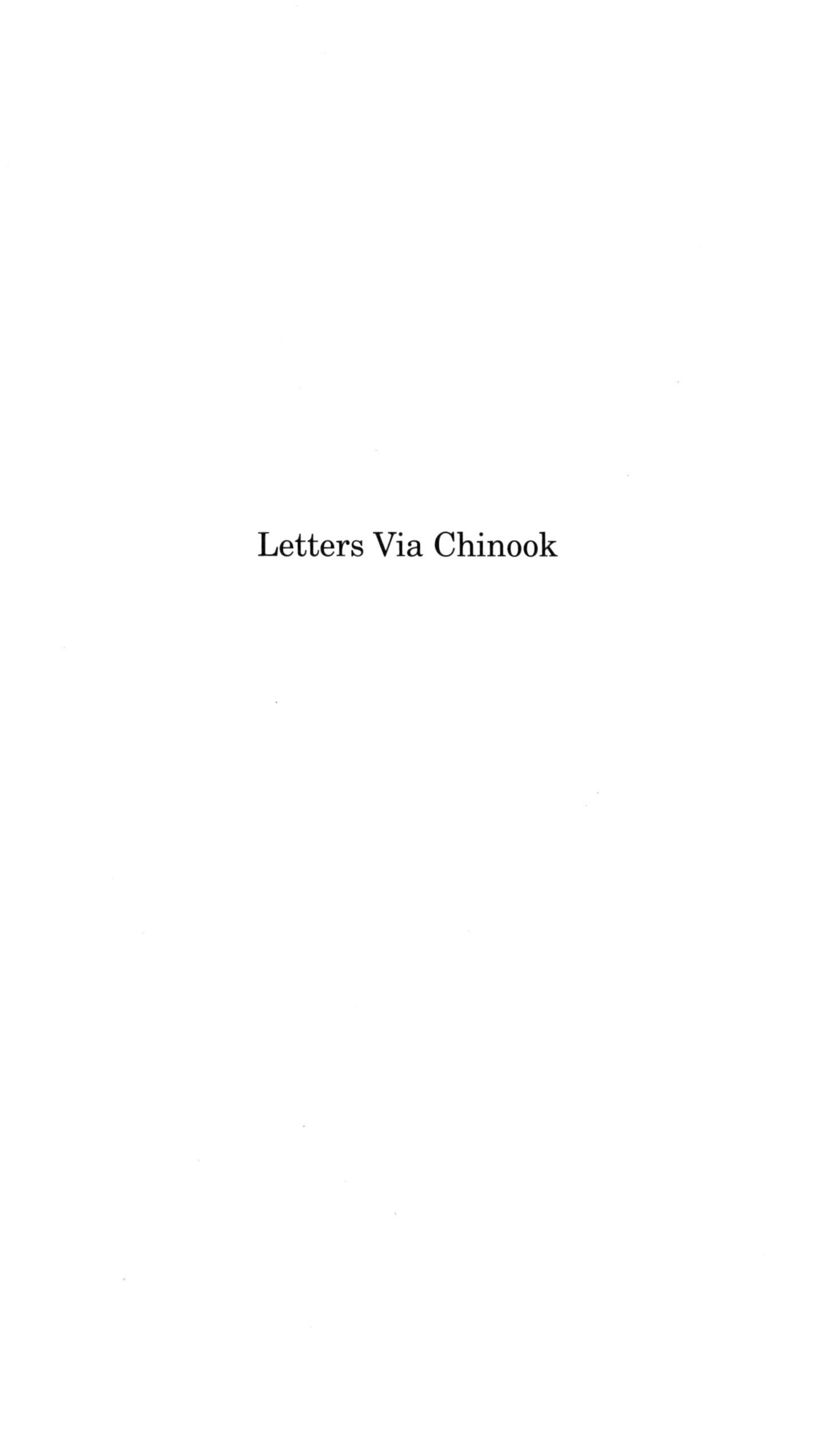

Letters Via Chinook

LETTERS VIA CHINOOK

To my Grandchildren
Laura, Brian, David, Philip

INTRODUCTION

I was born in a sod house. I grew up in a log cabin. Later in these letters I will tell you more about the home I grew up in. It was located on the prairies of Eastern Montana in Powder River County, eight miles north of Broadus.

First let me introduce you to the idea and meaning behind these letters. When you were born, Laura, your Mom and Dad gave me a book called A Grandparent's Book. That was a long, long time ago and I am just now getting around to doing something about it. That is because I am a champion "putter-offer". What is a "putter-offer"? It is someone who puts off until tomorrow, or the next day, or the next what he really should do today. I could use a fancy big word and say that I am one who procrastinates too much but somehow I think the term "putter-offer" is more descriptive, so that is what I am pleading guilty to.

I have decided that the book your parents gave me tends to devote too much time and space for some items and too little for others; hence I will use the more flexible letter format.

These letters are meant to be a direct communication from me to each grandchild. Some will be short and fairly simple, others long and more complicated. I will try to make each letter primarily directed at one theme so that each one can be understood without having to relate it to other letters in the series. Each letter will illuminate some aspect of my life but to get a well rounded picture you will need to read all of them. This is not merely a diary of events; it is also about ideas, goals, concerns and funny sayings. Read on!

You may be wondering who or what is "Chinook". The Chinook is a warm dry wind of change. It glides down from the northwest across the prairies and plains. It engulfs the hills and the valleys; it envelops the cottonwood trees and the willows of the creek beds. It creeps into the smallest nook and cranny. It loosens the grip of winter; the ice becomes liquid and forms rivulets of cold water running toward the sea. It sweeps down the slopes of the Rocky Mountains in late winter or early spring and spreads across the prairie grasslands. This offspring of the Wild Wind of the West teases the winter weary inhabitants of the plains with a taste of spring. Like Charlie Brown, they are tricked into thinking that spring has arrived, only to be dumped on by five inches of snow the next day. The Chinook is glad to be a postman for my letters.

These letters will tell you a lot about what it was like to grow up on a farm, sort of like a small ranch, in Eastern Montana; to ride a horse three miles to attend a one room country grade school; to drive one hundred miles as a member of our high school basketball team to meet another team in our league. They will tell about the hard times and the good times, the dry times and the times of thunderstorms and blizzards. There will be observations about the country and the people who lived there.

These letters will also contain some of my thoughts, ideas and concerns as I grew up and groped for a philosophy to live by. Random thoughts and observations, childhood memories and sage sayings may appear at any time; from time to time a letter will contain a whimsical ditty brought to you by the Wild Wind of the West which I will call a "Silly Symphony". A Silly Symphony is a fun rhyme that you can say or sing. Its meaning is obscure and only understood by spirits and elves. Let your imagination be your guide.

Maybe, as I get into writing future letters, Grandma will be willing to do some illustrations for them - I hope. Maybe she will even decide to write about some of her experiences in growing up in a big city, Chicago, and a suburban town, Wheaton, which were quite different from mine on the prairies of Eastern Montana. Grandma says her serious art work is top priority so she may not have time for the letters.

How did I happen to be born in the wilds of Eastern Montana? Let me tell you about the events that led up to this happening. My father, Henry Ambuel (the name used to be spelled Ambuehl) who grew up on a farm in southern Illinois, decided to seek his fortune by homesteading in Eastern Montana. He had been married before he met my mother and had three children, Madeline, Margaret and Francis. His first wife died when Francis (later known as Frank) was a small baby, about one year of age.

The family then moved to Chicago to live with relatives of the mother (the Welch family) so that he could have help in caring for his small children; but my father did not like the big city and did not like the kind of work he could find. He had left school at the end of the third grade and although he could read and write, he did not have enough education to get the more interesting jobs. So, leaving the children with the Welch relatives, he went West to homestead and ended up in Powder River County in Eastern Montana. The Homestead Act was a law passed by the United States Congress which provided 160 acres to any adult citizen who would live on the land for five years and make improvements.

In 1915 my mother, Bertha Preus, and her two sisters, Caroline (Linka) and Valesca, decided to leave Wisconsin and start a new life by homesteading in Eastern Montana. They also ended up in Powder River County. All three sisters had teaching certificates which meant they could get jobs as elementary school teachers. They hired men to build log cabins on their homestead property and took turns living with each other in these cabins, thus satisfying the requirements of the Homestead Act.

The Preus family grew up on a farm at Coon Prairie, near Westby, in southwestern Wisconsin. The three sisters graduated from high school and then took teacher education courses. Linka never married and continued to teach in southeastern Montana; Valesca married a homestead neighbor, John Gaar, in 1919. My mother and father were also homestead neighbors and were married in LaCrosse, Wisconsin July 12, 1917.

After the wedding the new Ambuel family: Henry, Bertha, and the children (Madeline, Margaret and Francis, ages ten, six and four) traveled to the new Ambuel home in Powder River County - the Henry Ambuel homestead.

The first part of this journey, from southwestern Wisconsin to Miles City, Montana, was by train and was relatively fast and comfortable. The second part was by horse drawn lumber wagon at the rate of fifteen to twenty miles per day.

This was July, among the hottest days of the year. If it was like most Julys in Powder River County it was "blessed" with a number of thunder storms, most of them dry. In the big western sky, typically in the later part of the afternoon, ominous, dark grey to almost black thunderheads would begin to build. Streaks of lightning would dart from cloud to cloud or from cloud to earth, perhaps attracted by a barbed wire fence, a tree or rocky point on the buttes. These would be followed by booming, earth shaking claps of thunder. These dry thunder storms promised water for the wilting plants and thirsty animals, but typically yielded only a few drops of rain and occasional pea sized hail. On rare occasions a real cloudburst might dump an inch of water in fifteen minutes. But cloudbursts are rare, dry storms the norm.

I do not know much about how this trip went; apparently no one kept a diary. I do know that in later years my mother took storms very seriously. She typically herded us into the cellar when a storm threatened. I often wondered how she survived such a trip.

Try to imagine what it was like to plan and carry out a seventy-five mile trip in a lumber wagon. I do not know if there was one wagon with a team of two horses or two wagons with two teams of horses We do know the horses would have to be fed and watered, that the family would need meals several times a day and that in the hot, July weather the three growing children would need drinking water every two or three hours. There would need to be protection from rain (if there was any) and from the sun. The five people would require toilet facilities several times a day - facilities that might consist primarily of a chamber pot and a hole in the ground.

There were probably a few farm homes with wells along this route where water could be obtained, but for the most part it was necessary to stock the wagons with everything they would need before the travelers got to their new home.

When they drove into the homestead and saw the cluster of buildings, Margaret asked "Which one is the house? Which one is the barn?"

That is all for now....Until next time
Best wishes
Be good
Keep the peace

Grandpa

P.S. From time to time others will speak to you by way of these letters. These voices will expand and sharpen your knowledge of the Montana I grew up in. The first of these will be from Aunt Louise who describes her view of childhood in Montana.

Letters Via Chinook

To my Grandchildren
Laura, Brian, David, Philip

This letter by Aunt Louise recalls her memories of
Life on the Montana Prairies

Henry J. Ambuel, a native of Illinois, came to Montana in 1915. Here he met Bertha Elise Preus, who had come from Wisconsin to homestead. They were married in 1917 and settled on Henry's homestead with his three children by a former marriage - Madeline, Margaret and Francis. Two more children were born, Philip in 1918 and Louise in 1921. The family of seven continued to live on the family farm until the children grew up and left home. Henry remained there until his death in 1940, and Bertha remained until 1945 when she sold her farm and went to live with Louise in Forest City, Iowa.

Throughout the years Henry did small mixed farming, raising wheat, oats, corn, and legume crops for hay. He also raised chickens, pigs, horses, and milk cows. The garden was generally the responsibility of Bertha and the children. Nearly all the food for the table was home grown except for sugar, honey, white flour and a few extras. Store bought white bread, brought occasionally by visitors, was a special treat. Pork, beef, chicken, eggs, milk, vegetables and homemade bread were generally plentiful. Fruit was provided by the family "orchard" which Henry planted in the "early days"; this consisted of a winesap apple tree, red and yellow crab apple trees, and, until hard times "done it in", a compass cherry.

Supplementing these were wild plums and chokecherries as well as currants, raspberries, strawberries, and husk tomatoes grown in the garden. Many summer and autumn hours were spent snapping beans and shelling peas for canning, cutting and coring crab apples for sauce, and skinning tomatoes for hot packing. A favorite activity was the annual outing to pick wild plums and chokecherries, used for sauce, jelly and pudding. Anyone who has not eaten chokecherries cannot appreciate the patience necessary to glean meager reward before spitting the pits. Nonetheless the family became quite proficient. Wild plums at first seemed a lost cause: small, astringent and tart, they defied anyone to make them palatable. But with the right amount of sugar and water, added seemingly endlessly, they were transformed into ambrosia, at least in the mind of the youngest of the clan who still longs for a delectable bowlful, laced with rich cream from the cellar. In those days no one had heard of cholesterol.

In midsummer the Ambuel kids longed impatiently for the first golden, juicy-sweet ears of corn.

So impatient were they that instead of waiting for the real thing, they picked young field corn to bridge the gap between appetite and realization.

Fall brought its own special treats, chief among them being the fat, green watermelons, so sweet and juicy they cracked when the knife cut through the rind. The extras were stored in the granary to be enjoyed far into the fall.

With frost came butchering, and nothing could be tastier than those first steaks, sizzling on the old wood stove. Fall was also the preserving season when rows of canned vegetables and fruit grew on cellar shelves, meatballs were canned, beefsteak put down in lard, and sauerkraut fermented behind the stove. As a rule Dad had neither time nor mind for household tasks, but cutting rows of corn for canning was an exception. This was also the time when potatoes were dug to fill the cellar bin and carrots were put down in sand for the long winter ahead. As days shortened and dark came early, evenings were spent with Mother reading to the family while Dad cleaned pigs' heads for head cheese and prepared pig feet for pickling. This was also the time for hams and sides of pork to be put into the aromatic smoke house for the annual ritual of preparing the smoked meat which would supplement the larder in the months to come.

One of the homey sounds of life on the prairie was the daily hum of the separator which, after both morning and evening milkings, provided the skim milk for drinking and the rich cream, delicious atop a bowl of pudding or sauce, and equally delicious, when thick and sour it was "sugared" or "syruped" after topping a slice of bread or a fat pancake. Cream accumulated in cans and was transported regularly from the cool, dark cellar to Broadus where it was sold for cash that helped to pay for the extras the farm could not produce. For five cents a dozen, eggs found their way into the marketplace, and for ten cents a pound Dad peddled extra meat from door to door in Broadus.

Broadus was the main lifeline to the outside world and the kids looked forward with great delight to the frequent treat of a five cent box of Cracker Jacks and the wonderful prize inside. Once a year the long stock-up trip to Miles City was undertaken.

The family was close to being self sufficient. Everyone had his tasks, and no one was too small but what he or she could do something to help out. In retrospect, particularly the happy times are remembered; there were, however, many difficult times. Some years the grasshoppers harvested the fields instead of Dad and the boys. One year Mormon crickets marched across the road in ranks separated by inches. Only by constant patrolling to crush to death the voracious intruders was the garden and nothing but the garden saved. The crickets were so hardy that even though cut in two, one half or the other would drag itself on.

Drought was a frequent visitor, and some summers even the garden was sparse, with potatoes at times the size of marbles and, even after cooking, almost the texture of marbles. Drought also threatened dearth of food for the livestock. Not to be outwitted, however, Dad harvested Russian thistles for hay - thistles which in the fall became tumbling tumbleweeds. How the cattle could stand the prickly stuff is a mystery. Tramping down a hayload of thistles was not exactly pleasurable; somehow the stickers always found a way inside shoes and under overalls. During these times of dry weather the pigs subsisted on cactus which was always plentiful; this was dug laboriously and cooked in a huge cooker to soften the spines. Such ingenuity meant that, even when vegetables were scarce, the family had plenty of meat and milk.

Travel in the first years was by foot, horseback, lumber wagon and sleigh. The nip of frost during winter travel was minimized by wrapping hot irons or stones to put in the sleigh bed. In 1927 the family acquired its first motorized vehicle in the form of a Model T Ford pickup. For years this served as the primary means of travel and was eventually replaced by a second hand Model A sedan.

Field work throughout the years was done with teams of horses. Grain was harvested by threshing crews which came around the countryside, providing social contact and excitement as well as extra work for both the men in the field and the women in the kitchen. In later years Henry and two neighbors bought a threshing machine in partnership, so the traveling threshing crews were no longer needed.

Cooking was done on a wood and coal stove; bedrooms were heated similarly. The wood was cut mainly from trees along the river. Dad and the boys for a time mined coal for the family from local coal mines; later coal was delivered commercially and stored over winter.

The family never had refrigeration. Food was stored in the cellar, and in the summer milk, watermelons, and other appropriate foods were kept in a shallow water tank built into the "pump house" where the water flowed through from windmill to stock tank.

Weather in Montana, as all natives know, tends to extremes. In the days while the Ambuel family was growing up, these extremes were not moderated by air conditioning or central heating. Temperatures in the summer could reach 110 degrees in the shade, and winter temperatures sometimes fell to fifty degrees below zero. One mitigating factor was the low humidity, so the discomfort level was less than one would expect at those temperatures. In the winter, water in the drinking water pail in the kitchen would freeze overnight, and frost would coat the hinges of the doors. Woe to the child who inadvertently stuck an exploratory tongue on anything metal in freezing weather! When temperatures plummeted in winter, lusty fires and warm clothing usually kept us fairly comfortable. Snowfall was heavy, and snowbanks bordering the paths shoveled to barn and other outhouses seemed to tower above the heads of the little ones. Among the rigors of winter were blizzards so blinding that you "couldn't see your hand in front of your face". In summer, outdoor heat simply had to be endured, and blinds closed against the sun kept the indoors liveable. The sod room was the favorite "living room" for the family both winter and summer since two-foot thick walls served to insulate the interior from both summer heat and winter cold.

Electricity never came to the Ambuel household, nor did phone communication or running water. Letters and visits were the only means of communication. Kerosene lamps and a gasoline lantern provided necessary light for reading and nighttime household tasks, and kerosene lanterns lighted the way to barn and outhouse. Bathroom amenities were supplied by the old galvanized washtub placed in front of the stove for the Saturday night bath, and by the "path" out back, graced by its two holes and an old issue of the Sears Roebuck "wish book".

For years clothes were boiled in a copper boiler heated on the cook stove, and hand washed on a washboard. Washing was an all day process, cut down to a few hours after the family acquired a gasoline powered washing machine. After washing, clothes were hung outdoors, summer and winter, and "long handled" union suits acquired their own character when, after freezing on the line, they came in looking as if they were invisibly filled with their owners' bodies.

Social life consisted of community dances (to which everyone came, babies sharing coat space on the bed at the home of the host and hostess), picnics, ball games, threshing times, and (joy of joys)

Fourth of July celebrations. Reverend John Duncan preached periodically in the Durst school, and sometimes held Bible vacation school there or carried the youngest Ambuels back to Coalwood for the week of Bible study and activities. Evening devotions were routine, and on Sundays when there was no church we had our own Sunday services of Bible reading and songs. In later years both home and community services were enhanced by the use of the pump organs Henry brought home from Miles City.

Medical attention was usually provided by the Doctor Book which Mother kept in the bookcase with Dickens, Thackeray, and the adventure stories sent by aunts in Illinois and Minnesota. When written prescriptions failed, the family relied on Mrs. Minnie Edwards who became an itinerant nurse when needed, and as years went by on Broadus doctors - Dr. Charles James at first, and later Dr. Marvin Amick. On rare occasions the family resorted to the Garberson Clinic in Miles City, and once to the Mayo Clinic in Minnesota; but for the most part, the family was healthy and local facilities were sufficient.

The family provided many of its own diversions: Mom reading to the family in the evening after chores were done; games around the kitchen table; late night reading by lamplight; community baseball on Sundays; hunting with the BB gun. The boys had skis and we had a sled. During winter "fox and geese" and during summer "holler if you're far, whistle if you're near" were among our favorite games; and when little creeks were rushing after torrential spring rains, great were the sailings that went on. Our rambles across the prairies were always preceded by Mother's admonition: "Watch out for snakes!", and indeed sometimes we did have close encounters.

Life on the prairie could be lonely, harsh and demanding. It could also be fun, happy and fulfilling. Money was scarce and the grown-ups often felt the full weight of worry about making it from one year to the next; but there was much to be thankful for, and in many ways we lived life to the hilt. Children were children, and as they grew from youth to adulthood, dangers were relatively limited. There were no hard drugs, and not too much peer pressure. Discipline was generally firm, fair and consistent. Life was not perfect, but those of us who grew up in that place and time are fortunate to have experienced the simple, tough, and straight-forward life characteristic of the Montana prairie.

Aunt Louise

P.S. Here is Grandpa again .....

CHILDHOOD MEMORIES: Cats

Louise Loves Cats...
Cats Love Louise

As a school girl she always had at least two or three cats following her around the ranch buildings. We had many other animals on our farm - at least one dog, some colts and calves, chickens, at times turkeys and guinea hens, and always those free loading mice and English sparrows. Louise liked all animals, but cats were the queens of this Barnyard Society. They were the most royal of the Royal Society.

We did have some very talented cats. One had learned how to catch a stream of milk on the fly. This was not a kitten. No, this was a mature cat, a Mama cat or perhaps even a Grandma cat. She would sit in our milk barn as we were doing our evening milking chores and wait for us to squirt a stream of milk in her direction.

When you milk a cow by hand you grasp one of the four teats, pull down on it and simultaneously apply a squeezing motion with the fingers beginning with the forefinger, then the middle finger, then the fourth finger, then the fifth. This motion propels the milk, which has been sitting quietly in the teat, out the end of the teat and down to the floor. If you are holding the milk bucket below the cow's udder you will hear the milk strike the bottom of the bucket with a tinkling sound somewhat like rain hitting a tin roof. If the bucket is partly filled with milk you will hear a gurgling sound like water running through water.

But I stray from my story. By pulling the teat sideways and pointing it toward the wall one can make a stream that shoots toward the spot where the cat is sitting. It is then the cat's job to position her mouth in the correct place so she can catch the milk. Our cat was very adept at catching the stream of milk, though on some occasions she did get more milk on her face than in her mouth.

My sister Louise, whom you may know as Aunt Louise, is the cat lover of this story. We were born in the same house, lived in the same home, went to the same schools, and played together for many long hours. She is contributing ideas and stories to these letters.

Here is one final scene to finish off the cat story. I am seated astride Chip (the pony who carried us to the one room school house three miles away) patiently?? waiting for Louise so we can get to school on time. Louise can be seen leisurely walking back from her last trip to the outhouse carrying a cat under each arm.

Grandpa

Letters Via Chinook

To my Grandchildren
Laura, Brian, David, Philip

What Is Montana?

Every place is a place unto itself. It is unlike every other place. It bends and shapes every living thing that calls it home just as it is modified, distorted, and sometimes destroyed by those who call it home.

Montana is a large place with many nooks and crannies to influence us or be influenced by us.

What is Montana?
Is it The Last Best Place?
Is it The Big Sky Country?
Is it the winds?
Is it the people?
The rugged, tough-it-out people who choose to live there?

So what is Montana? It is all of the above; Montana is The Last Best place: +4

The Last Best Place, a Montana Centennial book is an anthology weighing almost five pounds; it is a tremendous source of information about

Montana and its people, about the Native Americans, their legends, their stories, their spoken words and now their written words. It has observations by people who passed through but moved on, by people who came to put down roots and stayed on for months or years in the mines, on the farms, in the towns or universities; by people who were born there and then moved on to explore the larger world. It is a book to be read and re-read.

Montana is: The Big Sky Country: +4. Many have noted this odd phenomenon: the sky which is visible from horizon to horizon dwarfs all that sits on the ground below, even the mountain peaks. If you stand on the crest of a bluff struggling to engulf the vast expanse of blue within the bounds of your visual field you suddenly realize that the huge darkening sky is about to smother you as it settles down for the night.

The Wild Wind of the West now brings you a Silly Symphony. What is a Silly Symphony? Let me remind you, a Silly Symphony is a whimsical ditty, a fun rhyme which you can say or sing. Its meaning is obscure and can only be understood by elves and spirits.

Let your imagination be your guide.

The winds of Montana
They blow hot
They blow cold
They blow in the new
They blow out the old
They blow down
They blow up

They fill the saucer
They empty the cup
The winds of Montana - that's what Montana is: +4.

The North wind does blow and brings us white snow as it shifts the cold air from the North Pole to us. It nips at our nose and freezes out toes and makes us wear mittens and curl up like kittens in our snug little beds at night.

But the Wild Wind of the West is the Best of the Rest. It blows what it pleases from soft little breezes to a gale that freezes the tail of a kitten who has lost its mittens. Yes the Wild Wind of the West blows snow into drifts as high as the sky and up to the level of the elephant's eye. It blows the snow into odd shaped drifts around the edges of the tumbleweed and over the sagebrush and around the cactus. On the flat prairie it cleans the ground leaving nothing but the bare, bare ground and a few strands of Buffalo grass.

And then on a whim the Wild Wind of the West brings the Chinook sweeping down from the mountains, and as it sweeps across the prairie it brings the false hope of spring and before its relentless march it melts the snow and produces rivulets of water flowing down the creek beds as the remnants of winter seem to melt away. But then it changes its mind as suddenly a blizzard blows across the prairie. The snow blows and stings the face and freezes the breath as it leaves your nose and whirls around the corners and into the smallest crack. It finds the keyhole in the door and blows snow onto the floor of the log cabin and the animals hunker down behind any shelter they can find.

Montana is its tough-it-out people: +4. They are rugged and tough; they are friendly, generous and helpful, but reserved.

So - What is Montana? It is:

Its rugged, tough-it-out people
The winds of Montana
The Big Sky Country
The Last Best Place

That is all for now...Until next time

Best wishes
Be good
Keep the peace

Grandpa

P.S. Now that we have an introduction plus an overview of life in Montana by Aunt Louise these letters will move quickly from topic to topic wherever the spirit moves.

Letters Via Chinook

To my Grandchildren
Laura, Brian, David, Philip

Detour with Aunt Louise
Prairie Personalities

As an adult, looking back at the "tough-it-out" people who populated the Montana that I knew, I realize that it must have taken a special sort of person to leave the comforts of "civilization" in Illinois, Wisconsin and the other places from which homesteaders came and move to the "wild and untamed west". No doubt for some of them Montana was a disappointment, perhaps even a tragedy. But for many, whatever the difficulties and deprivations, it became a community, diverse and resilient, and a well loved home. It was the place where they raised their families and spent the best years of their lives; if they left they looked back with happy memories and more than a little nostalgia. That was true of my mother (your great-grandmother) who, when she moved to Iowa, never found it quite as good as the "Big Sky Country".

The diversity of the community, it seems to me, must have been one of the most striking things the newcomers encountered. My mother, coming from near LaCrosse, Wisconsin, had been part of a quite homogeneous Norwegian community. My father, (your great-grandfather) from largely German downstate Illinois and later Chicago, had no doubt encountered more variety in people and customs, particularly during his big city years. In spite of that, the mix and jumble of cultures and nationalities which made up the sparsely populated communities of Broadus, Kingsley, Olive and Coalwood and included our closest neighbors and associates no doubt meant quite a change even for him. In a community made up of Scandinavians, Germans, Russians, Yugoslavians, and others (of mostly mid and north European extraction) there was the opportunity either for the exhilaration of new experiences, or fear of and aversion to everything different. There were no doubt some flare ups and difficulties between neighbors; however in my memory there was little mortal enmity. The homesteaders tended to harmonize much more than they disagreed, perhaps because homesteaders needed each other.

As in any community, some personalities tended to stand out against the diverse background, or to occupy special niches in neighborhood lore. There was, for instance, "The Old Lady" with the three sons she raised by herself; her brother whose wife once said she and her husband divided the first strawberry of the season between them. There was "Old lady___hm,hm___" (not <u>the</u> Old Lady) "sittin' on the fence, tryin' to make a dollar out of fifteen cents". Not kind, you say? No, but not truly mean either. More like taking note of quirks, real or imagined, peculiar to all personalities if you look hard enough.

One "solid as a rock" neighbor was Mrs. Weipert. Her husband was dead and she had come to Montana with three daughters and two sons. She arrived around the time of the first world war and her sons were in the service of their country. Therefore she and the girls by themselves built their sod and stone house Sod was a favorite building material, keeping a room cool in summer and warm in winter. To my mind her house was as intriguing as a castle. We had a sod room too but the walls were maybe a foot and a half thick and hers must have been at least three feet. I loved to visit that solid, squat house and I think I was more than a little jealous of the fortress like walls. When Mrs. Weipert dropped in to visit with my mother in her neat cotton prints and with her friendly smile, she would sit and talk and nod, talk and nod, and frequently intersperse her remarks with a whispered "mein Gott".

Ed Gring was a bachelor with a handle-bar mustache who lived about three miles away along the Powder River. His log house was neat as a pin, and he was a dapper dresser. His place was a mecca for us whenever we had visiting relatives, since he had dozens if not hundreds of beautiful wood carvings - mostly of deer and other wild animals, horses with their riders, bulls, trees and other plants with intricate foliage. They were done as wall hangings, picture-like with most figures semi-three dimensional. Most of them were the color of the wood, unfinished or finished with varnish or shellac; they were professional and things of beauty. If you should happen upon a varnished carving (about two feet by three feet) of a horseman driving two bulls, with mountains faintly outlined in the background you will immediately recognize it. It was stolen from my vacated apartment in Decorah, Iowa in 1964. Of anything I ever lost, this was the most precious and (sadly) irreplaceable. I believe this was the carving on which Mr. Gring replaced the head of the horseman because someone took it for his likeness. I am not sure what that says about the man; was he excessively humble or excessively vain, or did he have some other obscure reason? Tragically Mr. Gring died by his own hand. He had contracted cancer, probably incurable, and chose to take his life by setting fire to a pile of logs, then sitting on the top log and putting a bullet through his head.

Al Waltz was another bachelor who lived along the river. He, like Mr. Gring, had a handle-bar mustache, bigger and bushier than Mr. Gring's! He was always neat, but not dapper, and his home was at the opposite pole of "kempt-ness" from Mr. Gring's. We seldom went to Mr. Waltz', though he was a good neighbor, and gave a horse to each of my older sisters. Margaret's was named Alberta and Madeline's was named Sam. He probably gave horses to most of the girls in the community at that time. I think I was born too late. Maybe he had run out of horses. The way we came to find out about the condition of the Waltz place was that he had the misfortune to develop a carbuncle on his neck. As I understand it, carbuncles are very painful, and he was afflicted with it for a long time. Perhaps he was away in the hospital; at any rate, the neighbors all got together and cleaned his house; maybe the first and last time it was done.

Finally I think my aunt, Valesca Preus, who homesteaded with her sisters, Bertha (my mother) and Caroline, was enough of a character to deserve honorable mention in this gallery of personalities. Valesca, like my mother, taught school. When my mother married she no longer taught. She had an immediate family of four besides herself for which to cook, clean, and on occasion to teach. Valesca on the other hand continued teaching after she married Johnny Gaar, a homesteader from Kentucky. The Gaars had one of nicest homes in the neighborhood, and an artesian, ever-flowing well. Caroline, who went by the name of Linka, never married and also was a school teacher. She usually spent weekends and summers with either Gaar's or us, generally some of each. Linka was somewhat stoical, and often seemed to have her mind off in the distance. Valesca was more lighthearted and vivacious, and I have been told an excellent dancer much in demand at neighborhood shindigs. Valesca's most outstanding quality, I think, was her absentmindedness.

Two examples I remember - one from personal observation, the other by the family grapevine. One summer Valesca and Linka had walked to our house from the Gaar's about two and a half miles away. When the ladies were ready to go home, Mom gave Valesca a bouquet of lilacs. However, as often happens with ladies, parting was slow and the visit continued for some time around the kitchen table. As the conversation dragged on I watched in fascination as Valesca absent mindedly picked off and ate blossom after blossom until only the bare stems remained.

I am not sure if Valesca told this next tale on herself or not, but here is the story I heard: One day Valesca, being home alone, was taking a sponge bath in the kitchen. (So far as I know, no one on the farms had bathrooms or bathtubs, except for the old galvanized washtubs only kids would fit into; so sponge baths were the rule). There was a knock at the door, and Valesca absent mindedly went to open it - in the "altogether". There stood one of the aforementioned bachelors. I've often wondered exactly what he thought.

Here for now I leave my "prairie personalities".

Aunt Louise

Letters
Via Chinook

To my Grandchildren
Laura, Brian, David, Philip

CHILDHOOD MEMORIES: The Outhouse

The outhouse of the frontier West was a toilet without running water. The basic structure is a hole in the ground with a flimsy wooden shack to protect any occupant from the elements. The hole is about four feet deep, and in a typical two-holer the outside measurements are approximately four by six feet.

This wooden shed with its roof is designed to protect the occupant from the blowing snow, the summer sun and the prying eyes of dogs and cats. The wood seat is made large enough to cover the holes plus three to four inches of overhang on each side. This platform is built to be about chair height so that when you sit down on the seat you will be as comfortable as you are in one of your toilets at home.

Openings are cut in the seat - one, two, three or more. Most family outhouses were two-holers, a few were one-holers, and a rare one had three or more holes. Once the inside structure was completed the sides, roof and door were built and the outhouse was complete.

A visit to the outhouse on a cold winter night tested your mettle and established your legitimacy as a frontiersman. A minimum of creature comforts were added to the basic building. Toilet tissue was a rare luxury. Instead an old copy of the Sears Roebuck catalog was placed on the bench and served as a substitute. A wash basin and a bar of soap were sometimes placed on a wall shelf or stand. A bucket of water with a dipper for rinsing the soap from your washed hands could be added - only in summer since heated outhouses were unheard of, and any water left in the outhouse would be quickly frozen in the wintertime. There were no lights in the outhouse; electricity had not yet come to that part of rural America. Light could be provided by carrying a kerosene lantern with you as you groped your way down the long dark path leading from the house to the outhouse. One thing was sure - visits to the outhouse were quick, short and usually peaceful.

A favorite prank among the bolder, more reckless young men (and a way to establish bragging rights) was to count the number of outhouses your group had tipped over on Hallowe'en Eve.

That is all for now......Until next time

Best wishes

Be good

Keep the peace

Grandpa

Letters Via Chinook

To my Grandchildren
Laura, Brian, David, Philip

CHILDHOOD MEMORIES: The Night We Lost a Road

You might say - how in the world can you lose a road? You might take the wrong road. You might lose your way. But how in God's name could you lose a road? Believe me it was easy. Let me tell you how.

I will begin at the beginning. My sister Margaret and I and her two small children, Jack and Sharleen, who at that time were about four and six years of age, had driven by car to visit some neighbors whom Margaret had known many years before while she was still living at our ranch home in Montana. That was before she got married and moved away to live in Idaho.

As was common, Margaret got to talking about old times and before we realized it, it was nearly dark and we had not yet started on our way home.

At first everything was o.k. as we were driving on some well used roads that were easy to see and to follow. But as the night closed in upon us, as it got to be what we used to call "pitch black", with only a new moon and the stars to light our way, we came to a large open flat area of prairie known as the "Moon Light". It may seem bizarre to suddenly come upon this large, flat region appearing among the hills, valleys and gullies of the range. Without landmarks and obscured by overgrown grass and weeds it was a perfect ambush for the unsuspecting traveler.

In this area the road was seldom used and the roadway was obscured by tall grass that came up as high as the hood of our car. But I am getting ahead of myself. I need to stop and tell you about "roads" in Montana as they were during the time I was growing up on our ranch.

When you think of roads you probably have a vision of a graded roadway with a paved surface or at least with some gravel on the surface. We did have some main highways like the one running from Broadus to Miles City or from Broadus to Belle Fourche, South Dakota, which were graded and had a surface covered with gravel. But the typical prairie road that ran from ranch to ranch was really just a wagon trail with maybe a bit of gravel in those areas that might be most likely to get very muddy, and maybe a culvert or small bridge at the site of a gully.

Roads were not really "made". They were produced, in much the same way as deer trails, by the wheels of wagons rolling over the open grassland as the rancher, homesteader or cowboy rode over the prairie and picked his way among the boulders, creeks, gullies, and rocky bluffs.

We soon realized that we were traveling an uncharted prairie and that we had "lost our road". We wisely decided to "camp out" in the car until the morning light would make it possible for us to avoid the most dangerous hazards.

It turned out to be a very satisfactory decision. The tall grass of the prairie made one think of the motion of a large sea. This starlit sea of grass was a thing of beauty, while at the same time an eerie reminder of the power of nature.

The children enjoyed the opportunity to camp out in the car in such an exotic place. We adults survived with only a few aches and pains from the unusual sleeping position.

Even Grandma, when we arrived early the next morning, did not seem overly worried about our late return. Maybe she was finally learning to accept things like this. Maybe she wasn't too old to learn.

That is all for now...Until next time
Best wishes
Be good
Keep the peace

Grandpa

Letters Via Chinook

To my Grandchildren
Laura, Brian, David, Philip

CHILDHOOD MEMORIES: Friends, Neighbors, and Classmates

I had many friends during my growing up years. In the grade school years they were either children who attended the same one room country school as I did or boys and girls who lived on farms that were located between one and approximately fifteen miles from our homestead, therefore close enough to form a group of children who could get together for summer picnics, Sunday baseball games, holiday celebrations and the like.

Sunday baseball games and summer picnics were among our most treasured activities and many episodes from the past keep seeping into my memory well.

Names recorded there include William, George, Earl, Dick, Elmer, Richard, Jack, Donald, Ralph, Guy, James; and then there was Joe, a sort of pretend friend with whom I could discuss and argue various points of view. Joe was not really a pretend person the way some younger children will make their pets and stuffed animals be friends. Joe did provide me with a method to think about and discuss various viewpoints. In these letters I may bring Joe back so that I can have a more lively way to present a discussion.

Now that I have written this portion of the letter on friends I am somewhat surprised at how much it is dominated by boys' names. I can remember a significant number of girls, some of them good friends with my sister Louise; but none of them stands out in my memory as being friends in the same way as these boys do. I suppose this is because, at least in that culture, things that boys were interested in tended to be different from things girls were interested in.

But let us return to our Sunday ball games. I remember very well how important those activities were to me. For a while in my early teen years I lived for those Sunday baseball games. This was real baseball (hard ball). On occasion we did play softball, but our regular Sunday games were baseball.

We did not have a baseball league the way you have a soccer league. There were not that many young people around and very few girls participated in sports activities that were considered boys sports.

On Sunday afternoon anyone available would go to the designated location for a chance to participate in a "pick up" game. Those who did not come were sick, away or doing some very important field work. Chores like feeding pigs and milking cows did not prevent one from participating in Sunday baseball.

This devotion to a game on Sunday (God's day) caused a very strong disagreement, one might even say conflict, between my Father and Reverend Duncan - an itinerant Protestant preacher who periodically gave sermons in our area of Montana. We will comment further on this in the section on religion.

After graduation from 8th grade I attended High School in Broadus. This was a small high school with about 100 students in four grades - nine, ten, eleven and twelve. My graduating class had seventeen students by the time of graduation.

Friendships during these years were almost exclusively with classmates at school, especially members of sports teams. Broadus was seven miles from home and I usually drove to Broadus in the morning and back home after school was out in the afternoon. Only in the deep winter months did I board in Broadus at the Miller home. Mr. Miller ran the local mill; Mrs. Miller was chairperson of the local school board.

As you can guess, the situation limited my social activities during these high school years. I did play on the high school basketball team and took part in track and field activities, so I had that opportunity to participate in extracurricular activities.

I have a hunch that the lack of social activity during these learning years was a significant factor in making me an unusually shy and inept person in social situations.

As I recall I never showed any signs of shyness or lack of participation on the basketball court and certainly was never hesitant to argue vigorously with my teacher or classmates in the classroom.

That is all for now...Until next time
Best wishes
Be good
Keep the peace

Grandpa

LETTERS VIA CHINOOK

To my Grandchildren

Laura, Brian, David, Philip

CHILDHOOD MEMORIES: The Night My Ridgepole Crashed

It was a mostly quiet night.

It was early August.

The gentle wind whispered through the tall grass, rustled the sage, and whispered through the clumps of willows and the cottonwood trees in the creek beds. In short, there were no threatening omens. So unlike Montana that the eerie feeling was awesome.

As I was slowly drifting down the stream of dreams there was a sudden crashing sound followed by scattered thumping noises that seemed to come from my bed clothes. Was it hailing? No! There had been no thunder or lightning! No sign of a thunderstorm.

As I shook the cobwebs from my brain and started to sit upright I bumped into a solid wooden object, equipped with splinters, only two to three feet above my bed. Was I dreaming? Was I, like

Dorothy of Kansas, being transported to a wall sized world of Oz??

As my head cleared I managed to squirm out of bed dodging the badly cracked ridgepole - as large as a telephone pole - that hovered about two feet above my chest.

How lucky can you be?? With another two or three feet the ridgepole would have crushed my heart and lungs and I would have been just another farm fatality.

That is all for now...Until next time

Best wishes

Be good

Keep the peace

Grandpa

P.S. Occasionally comments or sage saying will be added to these letters. Here is one of these. My mama said - now remember, a stitch in time saves nine. I have often wondered who decided that a timely stitch saved only nine. Why not ten, or eleven, or ninety nine? Who did the basic mathematics to prove that it was really nine?

Oh, well - maybe it doesn't make that much difference. But I do want you to maintain a healthy degree of skepticism - a questioning attitude.

Letters Via Chinook

To my Grandchildren

Laura, Brian, David, Philip

CHILDHOOD MEMORIES: The Crows' Caucus!!

I awoke this morning at five a.m. The morning light was beginning to sneak in around the shades. My mouth was dry, my tongue so sticky it almost clung to the roof of my mouth. I must have been breathing through my mouth.

A convention of crows was holding a morning caucus in the tree tops next to my window. I could not understand a word they were saying but from the tone of their voices and the vehemence of their argument it must have been about a very serious topic. I got to wondering - do crows argue about things like abortion and communism, fundamentalism, how many angels can sit on the point of a needle, religious freedom - or is all the tremendous discussion about, "What tree should we select for our overnight roosting place when the sun goes down?" or "What field should we choose for our afternoon snack?"

Since I do not understand Crow language I may have to consult my friend, The Wild Wind of the West, to sing me a Silly Symphony. Maybe that will reveal the answer.

In some mysterious way the Wild Wind of the West must have overheard my comments about the crows' caucus which then led to these musings about crows, geese, and Silly Symphonies:

Oh, blow ye hot
Oh, blow ye cold
But don't blow the wild geese out of the fold
Geese fly North and
Geese fly South
But no one knows where they come out

Wild Geese Musings:

Joe said to me: Are Canada geese smarter than crows?

WHY DO YOU ASK?

Well, the geese go South for the winter - that seems like a smart thing to do.

BUT LOOK AT HOW MUCH TRAVELING THEY MUST DO. THEY MUST QUALIFY FOR A FREQUENT FLYERS' PASS AT LEAST ONCE A MONTH - AND THINK OF THE ENERGY CROWS MUST SAVE BY WINTERING HERE IN MONTANA. AND THEY DON'T POLLUTE THE AIR BY BURNING ALL THAT FOSSIL FUEL. NO, I THINK CROWS ARE SMARTER THAN GEESE.

But geese conduct a symphony of sound - a real orchestra of the wild. What a beautiful thing to see and hear on a clear, brisk, autumn day. In March when they journey North they are the real harbinger of spring, clearing the way for the Wild Wind of the West; while crows - all they do is to make a lot of noise, a cacophony of sound.

AH - A TRULY MODERN TWENTIETH CENTURY SYMPHONY. BUT DON'T UNDERESTIMATE THE CROW AS A LEADER OF THE FUTURE. THINK OF HOW MUCH JOY THEY BRING TO A BLEAK WINTER DAY. THEY ARE TELLING YOU "WE ARE ALIVE AND WELL; LET'S HEAR IT FOR THE BELLS OF THE FUTURE."

Do geese do this bonding stuff?

THEY MUST; I HEAR THEY MATE FOR LIFE.

No! no! - I don't mean that kind of bonding. I am talking about the kind of bonding discussed by this fellow Lorenz.

YOU ALWAYS BRING UP THESE COMPLEX IDEAS AT THE TWILIGHT HOURS; WE WILL HAVE TO LET THIS ONE SIMMER IN OUR DREAMS.

SLEEP ON IT
DREAM ABOUT IT
LET YOUR MIND WANDER THROUGH IT

That is all for now...Until next time

Best wishes
Be good
Keep the peace

Grandpa

Letters Via Chinook

To My Grandchildren
Laura, Brian, David, Philip

Detour with Aunt Louise: Family Anecdotes

The Bowl of Cherries

One day Mrs. Weipert came to visit with her grandson who was about five years old. They stayed for dinner and for dessert we had chokecherry sauce. You remember chokecherries? The little black cherries about the size of a pea which are practically all pit.

The proper way to eat this delicacy is to carefully spit the pits. However the little boy shoveled down his cherries with gusto - pits and all. Then he looked up from his bowl and said "Mo', gramma, mo'"

Do you suppose he had a tummy ache that night?

Apple Pie

One Sunday the family, all except my brother Philip (your grandpa), paid a visit to one of our neighbors. While we were gone Philip decided to make an apple pie from winesap apples which grew on a tree your great grandfather had planted many years before.

When we came home, there was a beautiful pie waiting for us. We all dug in with relish, but guess what! Philip had decided to make this a really super pie and had carefully pressed the apples down so firmly that there was no juice and you needed a knife and fork to cut it. I'm sure we finished it; rarely was anything thrown away in our house.

Lemon Pie

When I was perhaps fifteen I decided to make a lemon pie. I liked to bake and baked quite a lot, although I did not trust myself with measurements; if a recipe called for one level teaspoon of soda, I would come and ask my mother "is this a level teaspoon?"

On this day I finished the lemon pie. It was beautiful and I was proud. I had always thought a lemon pie looks yellow and lemony because of the lemons. Boy, was I mistaken. It looks yellow because of the eggs! When we took our first bites what a disappointment!! The mystery was solved when we looked around and lo and behold, there by the cupboard sat the unsqueezed lemons.

The Drink of Water .. or The Stubborn Little Boy

When your grandpa was a little boy in a high chair, one night he asked for a drink of water. When Margaret brought the glass he refused it. When she turned away he asked for a drink again. Again he refused it. This happened several times, so finally your great grandpa, his daddy, said "ignore him" whereupon he began to chant: "water, water, water, water, water....". After enough of this his daddy said "throw some on him". Even that did not convince him to stop, and he continued "water, water, water, water," I guess until he wore himself out.

Is that determination or what??

The Time Dad Forgot Mom

Often Dad (your great grandpa) went to town by himself, but on this occasion Mom (your great grandmother) was along. Each went their separate ways to do their errands. When he was finished, Dad started out for home. Halfway home he realized he had left Mom behind in Broadus.

I never heard whether or not she got out the rolling pin when they got back to the farm.

The Time Your Grandpa Got Left Behind

One holiday, maybe the 4th of July, the family, and in fact most of the neighborhood had gone to Broadus to take part in the festivities. Your great grandpa gave orders that we would be leaving at a certain time.

Meanwhile we each went about our individual activities, your grandpa's being to find and visit with some of his high school friends. Time slipped away from him and he missed the deadline. His Dad was VERY ANGRY and said "Well, we'll just leave him here". (It was seven or eight miles from Broadus to our house).

I'm not sure our Dad appreciated it, but our Aunt Valesca and her husband, Uncle Johnny Gaar brought him home.

Aunt Louise

Letters Via Chinook

To my Grandchildren
Laura, Brian, David, Philip

Detour with Aunt Louise: Plants and Animals of the Southeastern Montana Prairies

Montana is sometimes known as the "Big Sky Country". On the prairies, away from the towns and cities, one can understand why. The vast expanse of grass, frequently unbroken by trees or hills, seems to stretch endlessly, with the overarching blue forming a canopy encircling the horizon. One of the delights of Montana is the beauty of the sky - typically brilliant blue with fluffy cumulus clouds floating in space; sometimes dark and angry as gathering storm clouds form; sometimes opalescent as the sun sinks in the West and night comes on.

Below this canopy lie the prairies filled with a sea of grass, sagebrush, and small flowering plants. Although one thinks of Montana as typically grassland, there are other features which vary the landscape and make it exciting: the pine hills with their dark evergreens; the rivers with willows and cottonwood trees lining their banks, the latter turning brilliant yellow in the fall; ravines (called coulees or draws) with smaller, broadleaf trees and shrubs native to Montana climbing their steep sides; buttes and hills, rising starkly from the flatland; and the cuts worn by water, who knows when.

Living in harmony with the native vegetation are insects, spiders, toads and frogs, snakes, birds, small rodents and, in keeping with the ecological balance, a few large herbivores and carnivores This at least was the harmony in the '20s and '30s when we lived in Montana. Today, as is the case wherever "civilization" has encroached the native species have had a rough go of it - though perhaps less so than in more populated areas with a friendlier climate.

The climate, with its ten to fifteen inches of rainfall a year and its extremes of temperature (up to 110 degrees in the shade in summer and down to 50 below zero in winter) dictates the plant species able to grow there. This in turn determines the species of animals which can survive.

The central United States had sufficient rainfall to permit the growth of lush tall grasses. As these grasses died and decayed they laid down many inches of rich, dark loam, for a hundred years or more producing the corn and other grains making that region the "bread basket of the world". Montana and the other Western states, however, with their sparse rainfall never developed the fertile soil that provided rich if not easy living for the midwestern farmer. My Dad (your great grandfather) used to say "With enough rainfall, this land could produce anything."

What "this land" did produce was a mixture of short grasses maturing early in the summer and providing grazing for animals all year round except when the snows did not permit access. I still remember how I marveled at the green, green grass when I went east in September to begin my first year of college in Decorah, Iowa. Grass in Montana was dry and sear by June.

Most evident after the grasses were the sagebrush and, mainly on land that had been tilled or otherwise disturbed, the Russian thistle, likely an exotic judging by its name. Sagebrush dotted the prairie, reaching a maximum height of three to four feet. Its woody stems and small, pungent, grayish leaves were not a favorite of most herbivores and it seemed, like its environment, to be somehow everlasting.

Russian thistles grew to huge, green, prickly globes, which in their old age broke away from their stems and, with the fall and early winter winds, rolled over the prairie as tumbling tumbleweeds. I do not recall being aware that they were eaten by the native animals. However when hard times came to our farm they were put up for hay and provided supplemental feed for the cows, as well as a lot of prickles for the unfortunate who had to tramp down the hay on the hayload.

The other major plants of the flatlands were the cacti, the most common kind being the low growing, spreading opuntia with its leaf/stems formed of pancake-like oval segments joined end to end, sometimes sprawling to a diameter of two or three feet. In spring these were covered with dozens of waxy yellow flowers, their beauty belying the beastly spines that encouraged one to keep a respectful distance. These too, in times of drought, were used as food for the animals. They were dug and cooked to soften the spines, then fed to the pigs which provided bacon and ham for our table. Whether or not other farmers or ranchers used cactus or Russian thistles to feed the livestock I do not know; but necessity bred creativity at least in our household. Another common cactus, and a thing of beauty, was the "pin cushion", a half sphere about the size of a half orange which in the spring bore lovely gold or rose colored flowers.

The river banks and the pine hills were each occupied predominently by a single species: along the river, cottonwoods which are related to the quaking aspen of Colorado, and in the hills pines, smallish evergreens unlike the giants of the Rockies and the western coastal area. The river which ran through our part of Montana was the Powder River - "a mile wide and an inch deep", sometimes in fact so shallow and dry that one might (almost) walk across without getting more than the soles of his shoes wet. It is a tributary of the Yellowstone, which in turn is a tributary of the Missouri, which finally empties into the Mighty Mississippi halfway down its course to the Gulf of Mexico.

In the late summer and fall we visited the draws and coulees, and the other rare places where wild plums and chokecherries for sauce and jelly hung ripe for the picking. The plums were small and tart, but with a lot of water and a lot of cooking could be turned into sauce, delicious with the rich cream provided by our small herd of milk cows. "Chokecherries" well described the black fruits, about the size of small peas and mostly pit. These fruits have a distinctive flavor and an astringent effect when eaten uncooked. They provided sauce for our winter eating, as well as juice for jelly and pudding. The juice does not jell easily, apparently being low in pectin, but when one is successful the jelly is delicious; and if one fails in that, all is not lost. The syrup resulting is a delectable topping for one's breakfast pancakes. and, thickened with cornstarch, makes a scrumptious pudding. We did not pick buffalo berries; however others made delicious jelly out of these tiny orange berries. The small trees on which they grew had gray green leaves reminiscent in appearance of Russian olive or sagebrush and provided yet another variation to enhance the landscape.

Descending the scale of size from trees, through shrubs and bushes, one encountered the smaller plant residents - the wild rose bushes with their fragrant, pink blossoms and the smaller flowering plants and herbs. In springtime the prairies were dotted with all manner of colorful flowers, some lasting into summer and fall, but most disappearing as the spring rains diminished and gave way to the drought of summer.

One of the long lasting species was the cone-flower or bitterroot (Genus Echinacea) with its stiff, cone shaped center about the size and shape of a bird's egg. The "cone" was encircled by drooping pink petals. This is one of the taller flowering herbs, reaching a height of perhaps eight to ten or twelve inches. Taller still is the sunflower which appears early in summer and remains through autumn.

Other spring flowers grow in abundance: bluebells; star of Bethlehem - the blossom a part of the fragile stem which rises from ground level and, like the petals, delicate and perfectly white with a circlet of green leaves at the base; wild geranium, grey-green and low growing, covered with tomato red blossoms resembling the flowers of strawberries and having their own special fragrance; gumbo lilies, a kind of primrose, also low growing with large, white, tissue-paper-thin blossoms about the size and with the flat demeanor of pansies; sego lilies, each sturdy stem perhaps eight inches high, topped with a regal urn-shaped flower. In its throat each white petal and sepal, touched with a splash of deep purple, made these among the most showy of the prairie flowers.

Among these flowers and the fields of alfalfa and sweet clover bumble bees buzzed in the hot summer sun as they gathered their loads of pollen and nectar. Wasps seemed to prefer the vicinity of the house and sometimes built their nests under the eaves, and in its sod walls. A variety of other insects - boxelder bugs, striped potato bugs and gaudy lady bugs with their kin the black beetles (who knows how many kinds) lurched through the forest of grasses; dragon flies hovered above the pasture spring while butterflies and moths, fluttered among the taller weeds; grasshoppers leaped and alighted on swaying stems as they sought the choicest grasses to munch. One sport of childhood was to catch a grasshopper, turn it on its back and watch it spit "tobacco juice". As I remember we had grasshopper "plagues" on a more or less cyclical basis; maybe at three to eight year intervals. In such years it was impossible to walk through the grass without stirring up a cloud of whirring bodies, and the fields and gardens were much the worse for their voracious appetites. Only once did we have to contend with the Mormon cricket. The summer these ugly insects, about the size of large cockroachs, invaded we did not have to worry about harvesting the fields. The crickets did that for us, and only by constant patrolling were we able to salvage garden produce.

Flies were a constant nuisance in summer. The only defenses against them were fly swatter, sticky tape which dangled from the ceiling, or poisoned fly paper sitting about in saucers waiting for the flies to come and drink. On oppressive summer evenings when the skies became dark and angry, these flies seemed to know something was different and would gather by the dozens on the screens of the kitchen windows; at such times, if they could gain access to bare flesh they bit unmercifully, mimicking their relatives, the horse flies, which were always mean and ready to draw blood. On summer afternoons when the shades were drawn against the heat of the sun and there was time to sit down with a book, the only sounds to be heard were the buzzing of big black house flies and the ticking of the clock.

Summer evenings brought a different kind of "bug". As supper preparations were made, or as we read quietly after supper by the light of the kerosene lamp, it was not unusual to be suddenly startled by a June bug (really a clumsy, bulky beetle, not a bug in the entomologist's language) hurtling against a window or the lamp chimney, knocking itself on its back then struggling valiantly to right itself. Small tan moths also were attracted to the light of the lamp, so much so that they often flew down the lamp chimney to their cremation. We didn't have a hearth, but often late in the evening we would hear a cricket fiddling somewhere in a corner of the room. Mosquitoes of course made their evening presence known with their high pitched song and we kids usually had a multitude of itchy bumps to proove we had been unwilling targets.

Spiders were around and about, and bedbugs and ticks were both a menace. Bedbugs lived supposedly only where people were careless, but even the most fastidious housekeeper could sometimes lose control. Someone visiting, especially if they had stayed in a hotel or place frequented by many people, could bring one or two in his or her luggage. The most careful inspection did not always bring these hitch-hikers to view, and from one came many. As the name indicates, these tiny arachnids chose to suck the unwary sleeper's blood and were very hard to get rid of once they moved in. When crushed they had a most distinctive smell (what good that information is I do not know) and the only other pests I can think of which are equally difficult to cope with are fleas. Our method of keeping the upper hand (whether or not we knew bugs were on the premises) was to dismantle the beds every spring, take them outside and pour peppered kerosene through all the cracks and crannies. It has been years since I heard or thought of bedbugs. I wonder if they are now extinct.

Ticks are relatives of bedbugs, and are about the same size prior to their meals - a little smaller than the head on a Lincoln penny. They are dark colored, and flat, flat, flat - so flat that when empty it is virtually impossible to crush them. They, like bedbugs, are parasites, and usually hitch a ride when one walks through grass or undergrowth. They then burrow as they suck blood, and in fact if not removed soon enough may completely disappear under the skin. They are particularly dangerous since they carry the germ (Rickettsia) for Rocky Mountain spotted fever, which is sometimes fatal. Usually, having spent some time outside, one watches for ticks and takes action before they become completely embedded. According to our understanding, it was not wise to remove a tick by pulling because the head could break off and remain beneath the skin. Our technique was to upend a bottle of turpentine over the attached tick, whereupon it would back out. It could then be disposed of by burning after impaling on the end of a needle since it could not be crushed. If a tick had had a really big meal, it could become swelled up to the size of a grown-ups' finger tip, and, stretched as it was, appeared no longer dark, but pale gray. The only ones I saw like this were attached to a cow's bag and must have been there a considerable time. At that point they could be squashed with ease. Presumably such a tick, if not foiled by the sole of a shoe, could loaf for quite awhile before looking for another meal.

There were enough spring and early summer rains to provide pools necessary for breeding toads and frogs, and mason jars became the indoor "fishponds" where I at least kept my catch of tadpoles. On summer evenings as long as the water held out, we heard froggie choruses from the ditches near the cottonwoods.

Snakes were a thorn in the flesh of your great grandmother. We rarely failed to escape on any kind of ramble without hearing the admonition "watch out for snakes!" There were garter snakes, bull snakes and the dangerous and feared rattlesnakes. The prairie rattlesnake grows to a length of three feet or a little more, and its pattern and color blend perfectly with the grasses through which it slithers. At the end of the tail is a string of horny rattles, a new one added each time the skin is shed. When startled the rattlesnake coils, elevates its rattles, and shaking its tail like a maraca produces the warning "don't come near me if you know what's good for you". Probably the rattlesnake mother, like our mother, gave her snakelings a similar warning "watch out for people".

During our years on the farm we had several experiences with snakes. Occasionally they would be found hiding under the hay shocks during harvest and sometimes a pitchfork of hay would capture one and it would be thrown up on the load. Once or twice we saw a snake (never a rattlesnake) in our "back room" which was built over the entrance to the cellar. When the northernmost building (the back bedroom) of the house was being built one of the kids heard a rattlesnake, apparently under the unfinished floor. Dad was away and Mother was no match for snakes, so she sent someone (probably Madeline who would have been ten or eleven at the time) to get Eli Severovic - a neighbor boy perhaps then a teenager. When he came, he removed board by board, and as he removed each probed beneath with a crowbar to try and dislodge the snake. Finally as the last board was removed, he found it, coiled on the rock that provided the foundation for the corner post.

Once a friend of mine was visiting and accompanied me on my trip to bring in the cows from pasture for evening milking. As I often did, I took along a hoe - mindful of my mother's usual admonition - and as luck would have it, we encountered a rattlesnake. As it started down a hole I caught it with the hoe just a few inches ahead of the rattles. I was not able to pull it out and the snake was not about to return for a friendly chat. So, in my bravado/show off mood (after all, company was looking on) I dug it out and killed it. That was my closest encounter with a rattlesnake.

Another time, also on my then-nightly chore of bringing in the milk cows, our dog, Mike, was with me and as he bounded over a big flat rock there on the other side was a rattler. The snake immediately coiled and rattled. Mike went wild. For several minutes he circled the snake, barking furiously. Then, being able to contain himself no longer he darted in to attack. The snake struck, and within a minute or two the venom began to take effect, and Mike lay down. I could see my Uncle Willie, who had been staying with us since my father died, driving into our yard about a quarter of a mile away. Somehow - I do not remember how - Willie realized there was trouble and drove up to the pasture; he brought Mike back to the house. The snake was probably long gone. The dog survived, but not without several days of misery. There was probably no veterinarian in Broadus, and if there was, we no doubt couldn't afford a visit. We had no idea what first aid measures to take, though I do remember putting some kind of poultice on his nose where small drops of blood showed the place the fangs had entered.

Sage hens and prairie chickens, about the size of small domestic chickens, inhabited the prairies, making their living on grass seeds and berries and probably the occasional insect. On occasion Dad brought them home as a supplement to our diet. Hawks during the day soared in the skies and swooped down to select their dinner from the rabbits and other rodents available. After dark owls made their presence known by their gentle "who-whoo", nighthawks by their plaintive "peent" and by the hollow whoosh of their wings as they plunged to catch an unlucky victim. It was said the black and white magpies could, like minah birds, learn to talk. Smaller birds brightened the day with their activities: twittering sparrows, bob-o-links with their three tone song; swallows in quiet, graceful flight as they busily built nests under the eaves of the barn. From the top of a fencepost the Western meadow lark, Montana's state bird, often delivered its distinctive notes. I sometimes wondered what this beautiful, yellow breasted bird did for a stage before the land was fenced.

Among the small mammals there were the usual house mice, field mice and gophers. Porcupines were rarely seen; each quill was a thing of beauty, but like the spines of cactus much to be avoided. If ever they became embedded in the flesh of man or beast, their fishhook-like barbs made it a real trick to get them out. Skunks also were rarely seen, but frequently smelled, and another of the local species to be avoided. Since they were nocturnal one seldom had a personal encounter. It was another thing to avoid their perfume.

The most interesting of the small mammals were rabbits and prairie dogs. Almost everyone in the United States is probably familiar with the little "Peter cottontail" rabbit. He lived in Montana too, but the kind that was really intriguing was the jack rabbit. As large as a very large cat and possessed of very long ears, the jack rabbit was a sight when, after being startled from his hiding place he bounded over the prairies. Though he used a different technique, one might be reminded of a kangeroo.

Even more intriguing to me were the prairie dogs which lived in "towns" consisting of perhaps twenty five to thirty underground dwellings. The entrance to each was marked by a small crater of earth, and often the occupants would sit upright by their doors looking for all the world like village folk come out to survey passersby on a Saturday night. If startled they would chatter, flick their tails and disappear into their burrows. As pesticides began to be used by farmers and cattlemen these little animals had to give up squatters' rights thus leaving almost sole ownership to agriculture and grazing and sadly the towns became few and far between. In recent years, perhaps because there are not so many farmsteads (much land being consolidated into large holdings and less cultivation) my understanding is that the prairie dog has to some degree made a comeback. Likewise more in evidence in recent years, and probably for the same reasons, is the pronghorn (the American "antelope"). Rarely seen in our part of Montana during my childhood, it has not been unusual in recent years to see small herds. These are the largest of the herbivores in this part of Montana, and are a pretty sight when, being startled by an intruder, they lift their white tails like flags and bound off into the distance.

Another resident, mostly unseen, is the bat. He, however, makes his presence known of a summer evening as one feels more than sees a shadowy presence glide silently overhead. Of course we believed the old wives tales: be careful or a bat will get tangled up in your hair.

Among the other mammals, weasels, badgers, and even wildcats were seen occasionally. As would be expected, there were not many large predators around. My mother came from Wisconsin to Montana and became a teacher in the local grade schools about 1915. At that time wolves were still occasionally seen. They, however, did not live easily with civilization, and probably none remained in the vicinity after my parents married and set up housekeeping.

Foxes, I never saw, but I think they did live in Southeastern Montana. Coyotes were fairly numerous. While one might occasionally see a coyote, slinking around a farm building in hopes of finding a defenceless chicken for his dinner, Mr. Coyote mostly made his presence known by his haunting bark. During the night hours coyote conversations produced a feeling of intimacy with the wild and at the same time caused chills to run up and down one's spine.

The largest predator on the Southeastern Montana prairie belonged to the primate order of mammals. This species came in many sizes and types, some with handlebar mustaches, some with braids, some with beards, some clean shaven, some with bobbed hair, some with hair coiled on top of their heads or at the nape of their necks. Their names were Ambuel, Rule, Ullrich, Watters, Rayner, Emmons, Mussetter, Preston, Amsden, McLees, Manker, Severovic, Gaar, Weipert, Raschkow, Schneidt, Paul, Hyde, Whalen, Waltz, Gring, Brock, Neiman, Edwards... And there on the prairie they lived their lives, raised their families, struggled their struggles, enjoyed their fun times. There they fought the climate, the weather, the grasshoppers, the drought, and the depression. There they sent their children to school, went to their dances and picnics, dreamed their dreams, and in some way left their mark on the land and on the future. There also, before your memory, lies part of your history.

Aunt Louise

Letters Via Chinook

To My Grandchildren
Laura, Brian, David, Philip

CHILDHOOD MEMORIES: Roughing It in the Homestead House

Daily life in our Homestead House was profoundly different from what you experience in your modern suburban home. It is sort of like comparing travel in a lumber wagon with a trip on a train or a jet liner.

It will not be easy, but I will try to give you an accurate and realistic picture of what it was like to carry out those routine tasks of daily living so that we could eat, drink, stay warm in winter and reasonably cool in summer and get some of the grease and grime removed from our bodies.

Our original Homestead House consisted of two rooms: one built of logs served as kitchen/dining room; the other made of sod served as a living room/bedroom combination. Later a third room was added. It was also made of logs and served for bedroom space. Other farm buildings included barns for the cattle and horses, chicken coop, granaries, milk house, smoke house, and outhouse.

In the typical suburban home most of the heavy work is done by machines and the energy required to run these machines and provide for the heating, cooking and lighting of the home is supplied by piped in gas or electricity easily controllable by gadgets that respond to the touch of your finger.

This is in stark contrast to the situation in the Homestead House. Every glass of water used for any purpose must first be pumped by hand from the well which is about seventy yards from the door, and then carried in a bucket to the house where it is distributed to the appropriate location - the coffee pot for brewing coffee, the reservoir of the stove for general household use, the washtub for the weekly job of washing clothes.

Similar efforts are necessary to provide heat for cooking and for heating the house. Every pot of soup is cooked on the top of the cook stove. The heat that boils the soup is obtained by burning dry wood or coal in the firebox of the range. We lived in an area where there were only rare cottonwood trees and willows along the dry creek bottoms. Powder River, three miles away, was the closest place where significant numbers of trees were available. In the opposite direction, on the distant horizon, there were pine trees in the pine hills.

Our supply of dry wood was accumulated during the summer and fall months and stored in a wood pile thirty to forty feet from the house. The process began by my Dad and us boys traveling in a wagon to our "40" along Powder River.

We searched out any dead trees that were solid (not rotten) since these would be dry and ready to burn without further curing. If the tree was too large for us to manage or haul we would pass it by. If not too large we would cut it down, taking care so that the tree would fall in the correct direction, that is it would not fall on us or the horses. Then the branches of the tree were cut off and the trunk and the branches were cut into appropriate lengths to carry in the wagon back to the Homestead House. Once the trunk and major branches were hauled home they had to be cut first into chunks, then split into a size to fit into the fire box of the kitchen range or heating stove. They were then stacked in a wood pile in the yard for drying. The final job was to carry these pieces of wood from the wood pile to the shed or lean-to where they could be kept reasonably dry until put into the stove.

Coal was available from some of the mines in southeastern Montana. At first we went to one of the local mines where the coal was dug out by hand or blasted out by placing powder into holes drilled in the surface of a vein of coal.

As you can see, everything one does in the Homestead House has a long, tiresome, physically exhausting work load associated with it.

That is all for now...Until next time
Best wishes
Be good
Keep the peace

Grandpa

Letters Via Chinook

To My Grandchildren
Laura, Brian, David, Philip

Detour with Aunt Louise: Health Care on the Homestead

People far removed from doctors, hopitals and medical centers get sick and have accidents just like those who live in the shadows of state-of-the-art institutions. We in Montana were no different, and learned to cope to the best of our abilities by means of the Doctor Book, mother wit, folk medicine and whatever professional help was available - and often this latter resource was scarce or non-existent. I say "we" though of course we kids had nothing to do with medical solutions; adults put their creative heads together, shared their knowledge and support, and made use of the medical practitioners who were at hand

In the years I lived in Montana - from my birth in 1921 until I left for college in 1939, and during summer vacations thereafter I experienced first hand this homestead expertise, much of it now all but forgotten. However, just as the knack of riding a bicycle returns quickly after long disuse, these

Letters Via Chinook have stirred memories and shaken loose some of the cobwebs that shroud the details.

During the time we lived in Montana I can remember only two doctors who took up practice in Broadus, a town seven or eight miles from us. With its 500 people it was a metropolis compared with Kingsley, Olive, Coalwood, Epsie, Powderville, Boyes, and the other small "towns" which consisted of little more than a postoffice and perhaps a general store. Broadus on the other hand boasted in addition a lumber yard, dance hall, hotel, school, drug store, barber shop and restaurant as well as perhaps 150 homes and growing. Miles City, ninety miles away, was the closest place where one could receive treatment for really serious conditions. On occasion the Mayo Clinic in Rochester, Minnesota was a resource of last resort as was the case when my brother Frank (then known as Francis, a name he came to hate because he was sometimes mistaken for a girl) went there for a hernia operation.

I do not know where Doctor James came from or when he arrived probably not until after both your grandfather and I were born, since each of us was delivered by a midwife. Your grandfather was delivered at home by Mrs. Byrd (Minnie) Edwards who for years served the needs of the local settlers. I was delivered by another midwife remembered by my sister Margaret with a certain degree of rancor for the fact that she slept most of the time she was in attendance.

My memories of Dr. James are very hazy, but he must have been in Broadus for perhaps five or ten years and as far as I know served the far flung community well. Dr. Amick was in our town through my 'teen and high school years, and he must have stayed something short of a decade, perhaps five or six years. Also part of the medical network was the Holt family who owned the drug store. I wish that some of the remedies we purchased there were still available. Particularly I remember a red medication reminding me of cherry juice thickened with cornstarch which did wonders for a stubborn sore between my mother's fingers. After several applications of this wonder gel it healed completely; unfortunately I have no idea what the ingredients of the salve were.

For years after Dr. Amick left, and in spite of valiant efforts by the townspeople, Broadus was unable to attract any doctor. The last time I had occasion to observe medical services there was in 1988 when on a visit I wrenched my knee and had to go to the local clinic. The clinic was small but appeared well appointed and efficient; it was staffed by a physician assistant provided under a program set up to serve communities regarded as sort of pioneer outposts.

Much of our health care came not from local professionals but from the Doctor Book. This had an important place in our bookcase which housed a more extensive library than was common in that time and place, with its volumes of Thackeray and Dickens, and the books which came from the aunts in Chicago and Minnesota nearly every Christmas. Home remedies were indispensable though sometimes getting well consisted of toughing it out until nature took its course.

Whether or not we "ate healthy" might be argued in today's diet-conscious atmosphere. We certainly did not have to worry much about "additives" and "subtractives" in our food, since most of it (except sugar, white flour, honey and a few other specialties) was home grown and home prepared. This meant virtually no risk from insecticides or herbicides; it also meant there was little adulteration or alteration of the foods that were preserved or eaten fresh from the garden. We did, however, live "high off the hog" on rich cream, milk, eggs, chicken, pork and beef. These products were almost always in plentiful supply, even though some left the farm to be sold to creameries or peddled door to door in Broadus for a little extra cash.

In those days "cholesterol" was a word foreign to us, and whatever nature and the family's sweat had provided we ate with relish. Thick sour cream on top of pancakes or bread was a frequent breakfast dish. Morning and night the whole milk from our herd of eight or ten cows was run through the separator and provided the rich cream and skim milk for daily use. Only in spring when the cows ate wild onions growing among the prairie grasses did we turn up our noses and say "no thank you" to our daily servings. The most favored meats were the beef and pork steaks available after fall butchering; however it was rare that meat was not on our table, at least for dinner and supper. Beef stew, steak, and meatballs were canned and stored in the cellar as staples. Some meats were preserved in lard, and lard and butter provided the fat for frying, cooking and baking. Smoked ham and bacon hung in the smokehouse for year round use. What our cholesterol levels and blood pressures were we probably never knew. Of course we all had considerable physical exercise which may have to some degree counteracted any ill effects of the abundant fats and proteins in our diets.

Vegetables and grains were by no means neglected. We nearly always had a plentiful supply of garden produce: lettuce, radishes, greens of all kinds, kohlrabi, turnips, rhutabagas peas, beans, corn, squash, tomatoes. Though we did not have facilities to freeze food for winter, we did can many vegetables, mostly peas, beans, corn and tomatoes. Fruits and jellies came from our winesap apples, crabapples, currants, strawberries, ground cherries, husk tomatoes and watermelons as well as from the wild fruits we picked - mostly chokecherries and wild plums. Wheat from our fields, cracked and cooked, provided the cereal for our breakfast.

We had the normal childhood diseases such as measles and chicken pox which usually meant nothing more than bed rest while the germ ran its course through the family. As medical facilities improved we had access to immunizations. We also had our share of stomach and intestinal problems, colds, and flu. During the flu epidemic of the First World War, the entire family was laid low. Some of the home remedies used were goose grease as a poultice for chest congestion; castor oil (much loved by the children!) for stomach/intestinal upsets; cough syrup made from licorice and sal ammoniac. Once when my mother had an especially stubborn chest congestion she used a kerosene-soaked cloth as a poultice on her back As I recall, it cured the ailment, but gave her an uncomfortable burn because she fell asleep and did not remove it soon enough. Turpentine was similarly used for chest poultices, as was goose grease. Running up and down the floor was one of the prescriptions for us little kids when we were constipated.

When my mother had milk leg a chair slid around the room served as her crutch. When I burned my foot in a boiler of clothes which had just come off the stove and was boiling hot, I didn't use a crutch - I hopped.

Not only were sophisticated medications and cures not available, the environment in which one was ill was sometimes unsettling to say the least. Perhaps the best example of this I can think of is when your grandfather, having a bad case of diarrhea, repaired to the privy for relief. I can only imagine - perhaps he can tell you - the trauma of hearing a snake rattle in the depths of the hole at such an inauspicious moment!

Minor operations such as tonsillectomies could be done locally, at least after Dr. Amick came to Broadus. More serious conditions, such as my father's kidney stones and the perforated ulcers from which he died, required the long trip to Miles

City where more sophisticated operations and other treatments were available. One illness which we seldom heard of was cancer. I can remember only one or two deaths attributed to cancer during my years in Montana. In addition we knew of a case of lip cancer, not fatal.

Injuries and accidents were not uncommon. Sprains were stabilized by stiffly beaten egg whites applied to the joint and wrapped with strips of old sheeting. This may have been more comforting than helpful! When a horse reared, pulling the rope which my father held in his hand so that his middle finger was pulled off at the first joint, the only treatment was to immerse the stump in a container of kerosene. According to him, he had very little pain. When I ran a rotten splinter under my fingernail almost to the cuticle my father cut it out with a jackknife.

One winter day your grandfather and I had ridden to school in Broadus with our neighbor, William Rule. This was because Philip would be away overnight at a basketball game and my Dad (your great grandfather) was to come for me after school. Before we reached home the brewing snowstorm had changed into something close to a blizzard and by the time we reached the TA (a ravine half a mile or so from home) Dad felt it was unsafe to try to cross by car. One of my overshoes did not buckle properly and sometime during our trek to the house it came off. By the time we reached home my foot was white, a sure sign that it was frost bitten. Today the treatment I received is considered a no-no: rubbing the affected part with snow. While Dad milked the cows, my mother (your great grandmother) rubbed, and when he finished milking he took his turn. It may not be accepted today, but it worked then; I have never had chilblains or any other after effects. Mild frostbite was not at all unusual - especially for Dad and the boys when they went out in the dead of winter to feed the stock. At fifty degrees below zero, one could frost ears or nose real fast.

Earache was treated by using a wad of cotton to soak up some hot melted butter, then placing it deep in the ear. It worked. Also treated with salted butter were stickers, boils and other superficial infections. The theory was that salt drew the infection to a head. My remedy for burns (such as when I threw a burned piecrust outdoors and the wind, catching the hot fat, threw it back on my leg) was to immerse the affected part in cold water until the pain was relieved.

Children and adults alike generally recovered, sometimes quickly, sometimes more slowly, from the various and sundry infections and accidents that came their way. There were of course some not so fortunate instances, where illness or injury resulted in death or near death. When my father was building our log kitchen the man who was to help could not come because his daughter, while ironing clothes, had knocked over a kerosene lamp, setting herself afire. She did not survive. On another occasion Mr. Gring staggered from his home about a mile from my Aunt Valesca's and appeared at her door very ill from a rattlesnake bite. He may have had first aid, usually provided by cutting the spot where the fangs had entered and sucking blood which would remove some of the venom. In any case it was possible to get him to a doctor and he survived.

There were occasional near calls when tragedies could have happened but didn't. The episode I remember as perhaps fraught with the greatest danger in our home was when someone took the kerosene lamp down from the shelf above the woodbox. The base of the lamp must have been cracked and no one realized it. As the lamp was being removed it broke and crashed onto the kitchen range which stood close to the shelf. The kerosene of course caught fire on the hot range top. Fortunately the fire either burned itself out or was put out before anyone was injured or the house caught fire.

Health wise our family had its ups and downs. All in all, however we were indeed blessed to be for the most part healthy, to have a number of home remedies at our finger tips, and at really crucial times to have access to what was probably as good professional medicine as was then available to homesteaders in southeastern Montana.

Aunt Louise

Letters Via Chinook

To My Grandchildren

Laura, Brian, David, Philip

CHILDHOOD MEMORIES: Religious Education - the Itinerant Preacher

My mother, the Reverend and I were having a religious discussion in our kitchen - or rather they were discussing and I was listening. I don't remember a single word spoken that evening but I can still feel the emotional tension as Reverend gripped my hand with great fervor and urgency. He pumped it one, two and three times to emphasize his point. At about this time my Dad interrupted the proceeding with "Oh, for God's sake, leave the boy alone". This did indeed interrupt the flow of the drama. I suspect that Dad by his brief comment did in fact save me from conversion. Who knows: without Dad's action I might have become a born again Christian.

Now I must make it very clear that I did not hear first hand any arguments or angry words between my Dad and the Reverend. I do not even know if any open challenge ever occurred between them. I do know that they each had very strong, deeply held opinions about the rightness of their cause. I am not sure but I suspect all of my knowledge about this incident came from hearing the discussion about it between my Mom, my Dad and other members of the family. It seems that at the end of the Reverend's sermon that Sunday (I have no idea about the topic of the sermon) he said he (and more importantly God) thought it was sinful to play games on Sunday. Dad was quite convinced he meant baseball. My father did not think it was the Reverend's business to make judgments like this.

The Reverend seemed to have the personal belief, noted in some Christians who have a very firm belief in their God, that because they have this they will get special protection - almost as if they are being compensated for their belief in God. My father noticed this in the Reverend one afternoon when he had accepted a ride from him. Dad commented later that the preacher acted as if God were driving his car for him, since he never seemed to be paying any attention to the road as he blithely cruised along.

During my childhood we had very little opportunity to be part of a religious group. The nearest church was seven miles away in Broadus. My mother had a strong religious background as a member of the Norwegian Lutheran community. The Preus name was prominent among the ministers and ministers' wives and college faculty in Wisconsin, Minnesota, and Iowa. She did what she could to teach us about the doctrine of the Lutheran church.

One of her constant themes was, it is more important to be good than smart. Being good, kind, truthful, honest were the important things in life.

She tried to read us something from the family Bible every evening. We were encouraged to memorize Bible passages. During many summers someone in the community would organize a "vacation Bible school" which was devoted to Bible study and the memorization of favorite Bible verses. On many summer days the entire group of Bible school attendees would recite in unison verse after verse. It was during these sessions that I first began to realize that I was maybe a little smarter than some of my friends. As a group we would be reciting the verses we were learning. When there was a breakdown in the group memory I was usually the one who carried on the recitation.

A bit later, in 1932 when I was fourteen years of age, the state of Montana as I remember it had a contest on knowledge about the flag. I won locally and participated in the state wide contest in which I came in third. Once again my mother's emphasis on being good and humble came through. You don't brag about yourself or feel smart about a prize. It is more important to be good. This theme carried over to voting for yourelf. If you were up for a prize or an office it was not quite correct to vote for yourself. This struck home when I was a member of the high school basketball team with a total of seven players: two seniors (Jay and myself) and five sophomores and juniors. On the first secret ballot in a vote for team captain, Bud and I each got three votes and Jay got one (my vote). To break the tie, a second vote was taken. This time I voted for Bud so the vote came out four for Bud and three for me.

There was one area of scholarship in which I learned early in life I was not a front runner - that was spelling. If I had been forced to get a passing grade in spelling I might never have graduated from grade school. This was as I remember brought home to me with a jolt, like being slapped across the face with a wet fish, when I was in the fourth grade and my sister Louise (three plus years younger than I) was in the first grade. The family was engaged in a play school session and Louise was able to spell correctly several words which I had flubbed. To a competitive young boy like me that was a real blow to my pride. I have wondered sometimes if maybe this psychological blow might have contributed to my life-long struggle with spelling. (Thanks for good secretaries). I really think there is a specific learning difficulty for spelling just as there is a specific reading difficulty (dyslexia), or a specific math difficulty.

Growing up and living a frontier life in southeastern Montana does not seem like a very promising place in which to receive a religious education. Looking back on my own life it seems to me that in fact I did get a very good education in the basic principles of the Christian Protestant religion - Norwegian Lutheran from my mother's side and the same kind of "ten commandments" behavior guide from my father. He was less concerned with the formal structure of religion, was not inclined to quote the Bible and seldom said anything about his belief in God; but it seems to me that his words and deeds were very effective in transmitting his religious beliefs at least to me.

My mother came from a family that was very much involved in the establishment of the Norwegian Lutheran church in America. They were ministers, ministers' wives, and some of them were active in the organization of Luther College of Decorah, Iowa.

Mother made sure that we learned our prayers, said our prayers and went to church, Sunday school and summer Bible school when they were available. Almost every day she read at least a few verses from the family Bible.

There were very few opportunities to participate in formal religious programs so the influence of parents on the child's development of a set of beliefs and a code of ethics was even greater than it might be today.

That is all for now...Until next time

Best wishes

Be good

Keep the peace

Grandpa

Letters Via Chinook

To my Grandchildren
Laura, Brian, David, Philip

Children's Games and Activities on the Ambuel Ranch

by Grandpa and Aunt Louise

In Southeastern Montana most of the farms were some distance apart. Our closest neighbor was about a mile away; most neighbors lived at a distance of three or more miles. Because people were so scattered, our "neighborhood" radius was perhaps ten to fifteen miles. It was therefore virtually impossible for kids to get together (except at school) on a daily basis, or for that matter any time during the week. Weekends (mostly Sundays) were the main times for any kind of entertainment, play, or association with other than the immediate family. Occasionally children might come along on a weekday when a parent had an errand but these instances were rare.

Saturday night events occurred very occasionally, and were mostly for the benefit of the older youth and grownups, although of necessity the kids were bundled up and taken along since there were no such things as baby sitters. Generally these Saturday night affairs were neighborhood dances. Local musicians (playing fiddle, banjo, guitar and accordion) provided the music. The little ones were bundled on the bed along with the coats, and the older ones tried their hands - or rather their feet - in an attempt to imitate their elders, or they watched or perhaps joined the smallest fry on the beds or in the corners. I still have an image of myself standing sleepily in a doorway, held up by the jamb, watching the scene. Otherwise these evenings are vague in my mind. I may have been sleepy, but I do not now remember ever being unhappy or bored.

Sunday in good weather and when field work did not prevent was the usual day to visit neighbors, generally unannounced. It has often been said that people in the West are typically more hospitable than in other parts of the country. Perhaps one reason could have been that after a week of isolation, seeing someone drive into the yard was cause for celebration. Early on, those arrivals were by buggy or lumber wagon; as people got more affluent (but never very), and the Model T Ford came into existence folks arrived in style by car.

It was not an imposition to drop in on someone, and often the day included serving both dinner and supper to the visitors. There was always plenty of garden produce in the summer, canned fruits, vegetables and meat in the winter, hams from the smokehouse, chickens available at a moment's notice, bread that had probably been baked the day before, milk, cream, eggs, and butter in the cellar. Seldom was the cookie jar empty, and often a fresh baked pie or two was somewhere in sight.

If you were lucky enough to have ice in the ice house the wherewithal for a freezer of ice cream was always available and many willing hands to turn the crank. This latter job belonged to the men with the help and supervision of the children. The women (and girls as soon as they were old enough) prepared the rest of the meal, but I never remember anyone complaining about the extra work. Part of the fun for the younger ones was listening to the stories the grownups had to tell during the meal. The culture of the day dictated that children were seen and not heard. After the meal of course the kids usually did their own thing, with their parents not having to worry about their safety other than perhaps an encounter with a rattlesnake or maybe someone getting careless with a BB gun. I do not remember hearing of a single serious childhood accident or injury in our neighborhood in the years we lived there.

Many Sunday afternoons during the spring, summer, and fall were dedicated to neighborhood baseball or softball games which your grandfather has already told you about. Sometimes the girls joined in - sometimes it was a boys' thing. But whether or not we girls were involved we usually found a satisfactory way to while away the time: by watching, talking Montana girl talk, or whatever might appeal at the moment.

When neighborhood children did come to visit, our play time involved pretty much the same games as we played among ourselves in our spare time when the family was alone. These were either board and table games, active games like hide and seek, or sometimes rambling through the fields or pastures - or perhaps after spring rains, sailing "boats" in the usually dry streams, or making mud pies. This latter I think was a girls' activity; I'm sure the boys would have considered it sissy stuff.

Because your grandfather and I were three and a half years apart in age, we played together a fair amount. Madeline was eleven years older than your grandfather (fourteen years older than I), Margaret was seven years and Francis (Frank) five years older that Philip so when we were small they were still around and we played some with them, particularly Margaret and Francis. However by the time we were in the first years of school, Madeline had already gone off to high school or to teach and as the other two left to board away from home during the school year there was less opportunity and - even when they were at home - less motivation to play with them. Perhaps I should say they had less motivation to play with us.

Early on our father put up a swing just outside the kitchen window. Swinging was a favorite pastime for both your grandfather and me, particularly for me, and I loved to be swung (as I grew older to swing myself) so high that I could see over the house. As a teenager your grandfather used his ingenuity to "build" a tennis court in the yard near the clothesline. This consisted of laboriously spading away the grass to make a smooth, hard surface. It was fairly successful, but the prairie grasses did not want to call it quits, and there was a constant battle with hoe and salt to try to keep them from taking over.

Swimming pools as such were virtually nonexistent, and when the boys sometimes visited the river or a gravel pit for a (probably forbidden) swim they took their lives in their hands. On one such occasion your grandfather remembers being with a group of boys at a water hole near the Raschkow's, some distance from home. Francis decided to swim across a stretch of water to a small island. Unfortunately he could not make it; fortunately one of the older fellows went to his rescue and averted a tragedy.

In the spring and summer, before we got old enough to help very much in field, garden and kitchen we spent time rambling the farmyard, fields and pastures, picking flowers, looking for rocks, hunting sparrows (and on at least one occasion calves!) with a BB gun.

Animals had some part in our play. For me, cats were a source of constant companionship, and we usually had an abundance of felines stalking the property. We had saddle horses: Chip whom we rode to school for years; Alberta and Sam who belonged to our older sisters, gifts of Mr. Waltz, a neighborhood batchelor. Riding was of course a way of getting to school, doing errands, and communicating with neighbors. It could also be done purely for the fun of it. We always had a dog, and often, especially when other kids were not around, the current doggie was a good playmate. Mike was the dog I remember most; as a kid I spent endless hours romping with him and sadly in his old age he had to be left behind when our mother sold her place a few years after our father died.

Chickens, cows, pigs and work horses, were never pets, though they played a big role in life on the farm. Pigs more than the others perhaps became a little more part of the family, since your grandfather usually raised a pig for the county fair held every autumn, and that required many hours of care and attention. One such piggie almost did himself in when, in our absence, he discovered a container of lard and helped himself generously. He recovered, but he was a sick little pig! Your Uncle Francis did not raise animals for the fair; he specialized in corn.

In the winter we always had a sled for sliding down the pasture hill and for taking turns pulling each other around the farmyard. Though we had skates that clamped on to our shoes or boots there were few places for skating anywhere nearby. One could skate in Broadus, and sometimes we tried to manufacture our own skating rinks by flooding an area of the farmyard, but skating was not a common wintertime activity. At some point the boys received skis which saw a good bit of use on the hill in the back pasture. Your grandfather also remembers making homemade "toboggans" out of pieces of galvanized steel fashioned as nearly like the real thing as possible.

Some of our favorite active games were "Hide and Seek", "Holler if You're Far, Whistle if You're Near", "Giant Steps", "Fox and Geese" and "Pump, Pump, Pull Away, Come or I'll Pull You Away". You are probably familiar with Hide and Seek, during which the one who is "It" must try to ferret out the location of the participants who are hiding before they sneak back to the safe home base. "It" remains "It" until he beats someone he has found back to base when that person becomes "It". Holler if You're Far.... works on the same principle except that it is played at night, so when "It" calls out "Holler if You're Far....." the hiders must respond either by a holler or a whistle, so "It" has a clue where to search.

Giant Steps (also called "Stealing Steps") involves a row of participants governed by the directions of the leader who "allows" all members of the row to move forward according to his commands: "You may take a baby step", or ".....a giant step" etc. The object is for someone to reach the goal line first, and it is perfectly permissible, in fact the object of the game, to cheat. In other words each person tries to sneak in extra steps or giant steps without the leader seeing that he has done so. If caught by the leader the "sneakee" has to go back to the starting line.

Fox and Geese is played in the snow which is tramped down in a big circle - sometimes two big circles with interconnecting paths. The circle is "cut" into quarters by paths (like a pie), with a den for the fox in the center. The fox, in order to get his dinner, must scout for the geese, so he runs along the paths hoping to catch one. The den is a safe place if a goose reaches it before being caught by the fox. If caught, the goose is eliminated from the game (and presumably eaten!); if the fox catches no one before all have reached safety in the den the game can begin again. This game could be played in the daylight but I particularly remember playing it at night in the yard with the lamplight streaming over the snow from the kitchen window.

Other outdoor games were "London Bridge", "Farmer in the Dell", "Mulberry Bush", and "Drop the Handkerchief". Defying categorization was "Rotten Egg". For this the "egg" clasped his or her hands under his knees. A person on each side then jostled him by his elbows trying to break his grip. If that happened, he was a rotten egg. Occasionally we tried our skill at walking on stilts and flying kites, both, as I remember rather unsuccessfully.

Hop Scotch, Mumblety Peg, Marbles and Jacks were quieter, mostly outdoor games. Mumblety Peg was played with a jack knife, blades open at right angles to each other. Each player stuck the shorter blade into a board (or the ground) and flipped the handle in an attempt to make the knife land upright on one or both of the blades. Different points were assigned if the knife was supported by the large blade, the small blade, or both. The reason the game was so called was that originally the loser was required to pull a peg out of the ground with his teeth - something I learned only when researching the facts in your grandparents' encyclopedia.

At picnics and special outdoor occasions other types of competitive activities were popular: for the younger set such competitions as "The Sack Race", "The Three Legged Race" and the "Egg and Spoon Race". For older youth and adults croquet (mostly for the girls and women) and horseshoes (for the boys and men).

Indoors board, card, and skill games were the order of the day and often the night and filled in what might have been idle and tedious hours. In thinking back I realize how fortunate we were to have had so many games as well as books to keep us happy and entertained. Some of these games the family may have bought as gifts at Christmas. However money was scarce and gifts were usually simple, often homemade. Many of our games - most of the names I no longer remember - we received from "the aunts". Some of the table games I do remember were "Scrabble", "Dominoes", "Pick Up Sticks", "Carom", "Checkers", "Chinese Checkers" and "Monopoly". Card games included "Rummy", and in later years "Canasta". (I got my fill of rummy when your grandfather, on orders of our mother, "entertained" me by playing rummy with me for hours on end while I recovered from measles or some such childhood illness.). Many of the board games we played were on the order of Monopoly - with dice rolled to select the starting player, and to indicate the number of moves one could make.

Pick Up Sticks consisted of maybe 40 or 50 pointy sticks which looked like very oversized (eight inch) toothpicks. Each person played independently. Holding the bunch of sticks in one hand, sometimes twisting the ends to make them fall in a more dispersed pattern, the player let the sticks fall. Then it was his challenge to pick up as many as possible, with the help of one of the sticks, until another stick moved when he had to stop. I don't remember if the game was scored, or if we played simply for the thrill of the skill.

Carom was played on a board about four feet square with a pocket at each corner. It was played something like pool, except that the players held the board on their laps, and had a "shooter" (one of the caroms which looked something like tiny doughnuts) with which he dispersed and tried to zap as many caroms as possible into the pockets. I suppose the person who bagged the most caroms won.

Parlor games could include larger numbers of participants. Some of those we played were "Blind Man's Bluff", "Hot or Cold", "Musical Chairs" (or "Going to Jerusalem"), "Twenty Questions" (also known as "Animal, .Vegetable or Mineral" and "Who Am I?"), and games of memory such as when one player began a list of items, the next repeated the original contribution, and added his own and so on down the line. This continued, and if a person made a mistake he was eliminated from the game.

You will notice that there has been no mention of television!!! With good reason! There was no TV, and truthfully, no doubt to the present younger generation's consternation, I think that was small loss. We did have a "Victrola" - a wind-up kind of phonograph (record player to you) - and quite a large number of records. Somewhere, somehow, sometime during our later years in Montana it disappeared. Perhaps our Aunt Linka borrowed it for her school and forgot to return it. As a family we played it from time to time and I remember during my teenage years repeatedly playing on it my favorite song: "Where the Silvery Colorado Wends Its Way".

We also got a radio fairly early in our Montana history. Perhaps the reception was not the best; on second thought, maybe it wasn't so bad. We certainly were faithful followers of a number of programs: "Death Valley Days" (sponsored by Twenty Mule Team Borax), "Myrt and Marge", "Amos and Andy", "Little Theater off Broadway", "Fibber McGee and Molly", "The Lone Ranger", "Jack Armstrong, the All American Boy".

In my late grade school years, particularly after your grandfather began high school in Broadus and I was being taught by my mother at home, life became somewhat more lonely. I was among the last of the children in the neighborhood, and not having a chance to associate with others in school meant that I looked forward with special eagerness to any cloud of dust which announced that someone was coming to the Ambuel ranch.

All in all, however, life in Montana was good. Children today might consider our lives deprived.

We did not. We were fortunate for the most part to have good health, to be poor but not impoverished, to have family and relatives who helped to instill in us good and solid values. We had good parents, a good home, good food, good neighbors, love and discipline, probably more community than most people experience today, and many wholesome things to keep us happy, active, and at peace with ourselves and the world. Part of this richness was - for that day and time - a wealth of opportunities to play and just be children.

That is all for now...Until next time
Best wishes
Be good
Keep the peace

Grandpa and Aunt Louise

Letters Via Chinook

To My Grandchildren
Laura, Brian, David, Philip

CHILDHOOD MEMORIES: The School Marm and the One Room School

She was middle aged with fading energy. She was what some would call "pleasingly plump". I can agree with that characterization provided I can say it with "tongue in cheek". She did not turn heads but tried to be jolly. She wanted to be a good teacher. That was her goal in life.

She tried hard - sometimes too hard. Like the day she got stuck in the school house window. This one room school building housed five grades with nine students, plus one teacher. There were no mice, cats, snakes, or black birds, but the bob'o'link sang in the nearby corn field and the meadow lark could be heard amidst the clover.

On this brisk October morning teacher forgot to bring her keys. We were on the outside with the only entrance other than a locked door a small window about five feet above the ground.

I was dispatched to a neighbor's house, where teacher was boarding that month, to find and bring back those wayward keys.

While I was gone the school marm decided that classes should begin with the students on the inside and the teacher conducting classes from the small window.

The children soon realized that they had teacher over a barrel (so to speak) and began to conduct classes according to the rules, regulations, and philosophy of the typical third grader, resulting in much noise and confusion. Teacher decided she had to get inside to control the classes so with some children pushing and some children pulling she managed to get stuck in the window, half in and half out. The children had had no problem slipping through the small opening but plump teacher filled the window like the cork of a wine bottle. With a final surge of effort on the part of both teacher and pupils she popped through the window and landed on top of her desk with only a few scratches and bruises to show for her experience.

THE ONE ROOM COUNTRY SCHOOL: Beacon of the Past? Guide for the Future?

The one room school is perhaps the most significant innovation in the history of Western education, the only format with a chance to compete for this honor being the philosopher seated in the shade of a tree discussing with his half dozen followers the whys and wherefores of our existence.

Let us begin by looking at some of the factors that led to the establishment of the one room country school.

Farmers of this era did not value education very much. Why sit around and discuss problems that have no answers when cows are waiting to be milked and chickens are clamoring for their evening meal?

Farm jobs must be done when the time is here. "Wherever you go, there you are". Rain waits for no man. The killing frost is the punctuation mark of farming.

The population is sparse. The critical combustion point must await the right mixture of energy, enthusiasm and intellectual curiosity before the learning atmosphere achieves a flash point and a cloudburst occurs. When that cloudburst occurs the one room school is born.

The impact of the one room school system is more than the sum of its parts: the total is made up of all one room school teachers and a mixture of youth and enthusiasm plus middle aged calm and reassurance. Don't smother me with your facts - show me their significance.

The use of this format has largely disappeared from the American educational scene, much to the detriment of our children's education. Perhaps we should look for ways to recapture some of the advantages provided by the one room school.

What were some of those advantages? Some have said that the one room school provides each child with one year of schooling and sixteen years of review. By the time the eighth grader graduates he has had a review of the same material at least sixteen times. If he did not quite get it the first time he has a chance to get a better understanding on the second, third, and fourth time through.

He has also heard a number of wrong answers, and conflicting interpretations. The world does not come to an end because teacher or pupil is wrong. If the teacher gets something wrong as she explains a science problem to the fifth grader, the third grader may burst in with the correct summary or answer. The first grader sometimes has a better answer than the eighth grader. The bright second grader can sometimes give the confused sixth grader a better understanding than the teacher. The gentle middle aged teacher makes failure seem more acceptable.

In addition to learning the three R's and some basic science concepts each child gets to observe some significant social interaction between the older and younger children and between the teacher and pupils.

When the somewhat disruptive and stubborn fourth grader begins to cause trouble, teacher can quickly ask his help cleaning the black board, carrying out the ashes, or bringing in new firewood. Usually there are enough chores to occupy the time of all the children in the school. The child learns that the teacher's request for assistance from an obstreperous sixth grader can have a great calming effect on the classroom atmosphere. In a one room school there are many social skills to be observed and learned.

YEARNINGS: The Young School Marm and the one Room Country School

She is young, pretty, perky and full of vim and vigor. This is her first year as a teacher in a country school. Her enthusiasm more than makes up for her lack of experience. When her musical skills and training produce a children's chorus capable of putting on a Christmas program of holiday songs for the Christmas celebration her place in the community is assured. Later the same year a male quartet participates in the Easter program. Even in rural America there is some desire for cultural and artistic expression. This young teacher awakened these artistic yearnings in the members of the community and some romantic feelings in some of the young men of the area. Some of the older boys in the school may have experienced their first teacher crush.

Most teachers in these country schools were women, many approaching middle age. When they came to the frontier areas some of them were no doubt hoping to get married. These fairly mature women were responsible for considerable cultural stimulation and socialization, more than is generally recognized. Another large group were recent graduates of teacher education (normal) schools. Many of these married and became permanent members of the community.

The influence of all these one room country school teachers on the development of the life and the socialization of the frontier must have been immense. I do not know of any studies about the subject, nor do I know any studies which have attempted to evaluate the effectiveness of the one room school.

How can we capture some of the values and the unique role of the one room school? That is not very clear. What I am suggesting is a two class room experience: first a typical class room experience to be fit into standard age slots and second a multi-grade classroom — say with grades one, two, three and four or grades two, three, four and five.

Class one would have typical classroom teaching. Class two would be multigrade and, in addition to the standardized classes, would meet to choose, plan and carry out a project or topic such as build a playground for the school, plan and carry out a musical presentation, plan and present a play, plan and put on an art show, plan and conduct an election for class officers.

I suggest that the question of the value of the one room school could be studied by: having each child participate in (S) the standard classroom only or (E) a standard classroom plus experimental, multigrade classroom. The E students would have a standard curriculum four days a week, then get to participate one day each week in classes made up of, say, the ages six, seven, eight, and nine. This second class on the fifth day would be devoted to selecting a problem or project and would attempt to evaluate the learning of such skills as conflict resolution and how to make the democratic process work.

That is all for now...Until next time
Best wishes
Be good
Keep the peace

Grandpa

Grandma Preus with three Preus sisters (L-R Bertha, Paula, Valesca) outside homestead cabin. About 1916.

Bertha Preus Ambuel's ready made family of three with their new baby brother Philip outside sod room of the Ambuel homestead, 1918. L-R Margaret, Madeline, Francis.

Henry Ambuel's children by his first marriage, 1919.
L-R Francis, Margaret, Madeline.

Francis and Philip, 1920.

Philip outside kitchen window, 1920.

Standing L-R Margaret, Francis, Madeline, Bertha; sitting, L-R Johnny Gaar, Henry with Philip. 1920 or 1921.

The Ambuel family, 1922. Left to right: Margaret, Francis, Madeline, Philip, Henry, Bertha and Louise.

Bertha, Henry and Mike.

Madeline at high school graduation, 1925.

At coal mine; L-R Henry, ?, Louise, Margaret about 1928.

A new family of kittens. L-R Louise, Philip, Francis, about 1926.

Philip with his pig, about 1926.

Francis with his corn, 1926.

Louise with her cats, about 1928.

Henry and Bertha at the grindstone. North room of house in background. Notice grass growing on sod roof.

Valesca and Johnny Gaar outside their home.

Durst school house. Probably last day of vacation school, about 1928.

Durst school, 1930. L-R Front row: Betty Emmons, Johnny Mussetter, Frieda Ullrich, Louise Ambuel, Kermit Edwards. Middle row: Charley Mussetter, Maymie Mussetter, Carl Ullrich. Back row: Philip Ambuel, Gertrude Ullrich, James Mussetter, Kenneth Edwards, Mrs. Nash.

Durst school, 1932. L-R Front row: Louise Ambuel, Johnny Mussetter, Frieda Ullrich, Chester Mussetter. Back Row: Maymie Mussetter, Evelyn Cole (teacher), Philip Ambuel, probably Carl Ullrich, Charley Mussetter.

Ambuel farmstead looking northwest, about 1937. From left: privy, smoke-house, house (kitchen, sod room bedrooms), well house and windmill, Model A Ford.

Mrs. Weipert with son George.

One of Mr. Gring's carvings. Figure may represent Mr. Gring.

Al Waltz

Valesca Gaar

Prairie Personalities

Small community gathering. L-R Front row: Esther Mae Rayner, Grandma Rayner, Bertha Ambuel, Dorothy Rayner, Billy Rayner. Second row: Mrs. Lee Rayner, Lee Rayner, Mrs. Frank Watters, Mrs. Ralph Amsden, Rosine Preus Moen, Paula Preus, Valesca Gaar, Johnny Gaar. Back row: Henry Ambuel, Will Preus, Caroline Preus.

Large community gathering.

Phyllis and Mike Landa, current owners of Ambuel homestead, 1988.

Carl Ullrich at Landa's, the old Al Waltz place, in 1988 .

Philip on rock just south of Broadus: "...the sense of vast horizons...things yet remaining to be explored," 1980.

LETTERS VIA CHINOOK

To My Grandchildren
Laura, Brian, David, Philip

CHILDHOOD MEMORIES: Hard Times

Being a homesteader rancher on the frontier of Eastern Montana was never an easy lot. Homesteaders were under the threat of hard times - hard times both from physical and emotional standpoints. There was the threat of hard physical labor, blizzards, hailstorms, sub-zero winters, summer temperatures reaching the 110s or above, grasshoppers, Mormon crickets, and the constant threat of drought. But the real threat was the double whammy of drought and depression. This is in marked contrast to the rosy picture projected in the propaganda brochures put out by the railroad companies as they were trying to sell the new Western frontier to potential homesteaders from the east and midwest.

The emotional strain of living under the constant threat of failure and physical injury was profoundly added to by the loneliness and lack of stimulation through social contacts. This was especially true for the women. I can remember how my mother said at times she felt like going into the front yard and screaming.

Drought is a constant threat to the farmer of southeastern Montana. If the dry period is very severe or lasts too long, for example two to three years running, drought all by itself is enough to ruin the farmer of the area. However if there is enough feed left from last year's harvest to tide the farmer and his animals over for another year, then drought alone may not ruin him. When drought and depression come at the same time, however, then the farmer has no way to hold his head above the onslaught of the drought.

My father tried several not so successful techniques to pull him through the hard times. One such technique was to feed cactus to the livestock. Cactus is a good dry-climate plant and certain types will flourish in the dry areas of southeastern Montana. There is one big problem: cactus plants carry a formidable armament of very sharp spines to protect them against the plant eating animals of the semi desert. Dad would harvest a number of cactus plants, cook them in an iron pot until the sharp spines were soft and then feed them to our pigs. This was a fine idea and worked except for one thing. It is very labor intensive and wore out Dad and the boys long before the pigs were adequately fed.

At another time Dad tried to feed chopped up pumpkins and squash to our hungry cows; pumpkins are a relatively good semi-arid crop. But on two occasions that I am aware of the cows choked on the pumpkin pieces and died of asphyxiation. Cows are apparently not equipped to eat chunks of food just as a small child is not equipped to eat things like peanuts and chunks or sticks of carrots.

The so-called Russian thistles (tumble weeds) grow well in southeastern Montana and are gladly consumed by cattle. There is one problem - the laxative effect: too much thistle leads to too much diarrhea just like too many prunes leads to too many trips to the toilet.

Of all the hard times my Dad had to struggle through, most of which I knew nothing about, one incident stands out vividly in my memory. I believe this occurred in 1928, the depth of the Great Depression. In that year President Roosevelt initiated a program to buy farm livestock to take them off the market thus removing them from and propping up the market. Dad had four or five yearling steers which could not be sold. Conditions were so bad that the farm markets in the midwest simply had no buyers willing to bid on this kind of animal. That same summer had been a disaster because of the severe drought. If this had been even an average dry year he would have had enough hay to feed these five steers in addition to the milk cows. He had enough hay for the milk cows, but the steers would not have lived through the winter, so the only option left for Dad was to sell to the government program. The government buyer carefully looked over the five healthy, vigorous young animals and then made his offer: $10.00 per head!!

Just a year before these same steers would have sold for $100 per head.

The double whammy of drought and depression were the major threats to the survival of the homesteader, but we experienced other occasions of near disaster as well. One year we had an invasion of Mormon crickets. At one stage the crickets literally produced a solid blanket over the garden and fields. One year the grasshoppers stripped the growing plants of all their leaves; and we had several severe hailstorms that threatened total destruction but barely missed our property.

Hard times were a constant companion of the homesteader; but there were many experiences to balance these grim times. The fun times included experiencing the beauty of the spring flowers, especially wild roses; excursions to pick cherries and plums; community picnics; and little personal incidents as illustrated by our Chokecherry Kid.

That is all for now...Until next time
Best wishes
Be good
Keep the peace

Grandpa

The Chokecherry Kid

We called him the chokecherry kid. You know what chokecherries are: those small, miserly, sour cherries that grow along the dry creek beds on the prairies of Eastern Montana and are used, with much sugar and water added, to give a pleasant tang to jellies and jams.

The typical chokecherry is made up of a pit, three to four millimeters in diameter, surrounded by the fleshy part of the cherry which is maybe one and a half to two millimeters in thickness. Getting the fleshy portion of the cherry free from the pit is very labor intensive.

But - not for the chokecherry kid! He was a five year old grandson of our neighbor, Mrs. Weipert. A spoonful of chokecherry sauce, pits and all, would disappear down his gullet in a flash as he kept saying "Mo, Grandma, mo".

Letters Via Chinook

To My Grandchildren
Laura, Brian, David, Philip

Detour With Aunt Louise: Holidays, Celebrations, and Community Events

Homesteaders in Montana celebrated holidays probably much like people in other parts of the country, although perhaps in a simpler way. Holidays such as Easter, Thanksgiving, and Christmas tended to be family affairs, and because only a few relatives lived close enough to participate, mostly included immediate family. For us this generally meant the three Preus sisters and our family: Valesca and Johnnie Gaar who had no children; Caroline (Linka) who did not marry but spent her school holidays with us or Gaars, and our family of seven: Mom (Bertha), Dad (Henry), Madeline, Margaret, and Francis (half siblings from Dad's first marriage in Illinois), and Philip and Louise born respectively one and four years after the Preus/Ambuel wedding in LaCrosse, Wisconsin. I do not recall friends or neighbors being included in such gatherings. They hopefully were occupied in their own homes, with their own relatives.

I recall occasional special programs or services which occurred at the school house, since there was no church building in the community. Because the Reverend John Duncan served a far flung flock no community could be assured of having a religious service on a holiday. Due to the sparse population the Methodist and Congregational churches cooperated by not overlapping their pastoral assignments; even regular Sunday services were spasmodic, available no more than once a month. Sometimes the school teacher served as the mover and shaker for special events - on one occasion assembling a male quartet from the neighborhood to put on an Easter "cantata". Frequently at Christmas the school presented a program of children's songs, recitations and playlets.

All of the country school teachers during my childhood were women and each put her own stamp on whatever event occurred. Miss Leamon was the teacher when I was in first grade and I do not remember much about her tenure except that I must have liked her. For Christmas that year I received from somewhere a long legged cloth doll of the sort then popular as a pajama bag to add class when displayed on one's bed. I guess I didn't care too much for the doll, and the family seemed to think it was not all that appropriate for a child of six, so they suggested I give it to Madeline; instead I voted to give it to Miss Leamon.

During my second year Miss Peterson was our teacher and (I believe) it was she who for the Christmas program transformed our little one room school into a veritable fairyland. I cannot now describe the decorations, but to my childish eyes entering the door that night was like stepping into a storybook dreamland. Mrs. Pearl Nash taught in the Durst school during my third grade and I do not remember what programs we had during that year though I do remember that we had the unusually large number of twelve children attending the Durst school. During my fourth and fifth grades Miss Cole was our teacher. Her forte was music and it was she who molded our Dad, John Severovic, and probably Herman Ullrich and Mr. Mussetter into a passable quartet for the Easter program.

I spent most of my sixth, seventh, and eighth grades at home, with my mother as teacher. This was because Philip (your grandfather) by that time had graduated from grade school and it did not seem feasible for a twelve year old girl to ride horseback alone to a school three miles from home, particularly since winter blizzards could be horrendous and my father's health was not good. During those years I therefore had no opportunity to participate in any school related special events.

For Easter and Thanksgiving our celebration primarily centered around company and a special dinner: potatoes, meat (usually chicken - one or two years turkey when we unsuccessfully experimented with raising gobblers), Mom's bread dressing baked separate from the bird, cranberry sauce for Thanksgiving, a variety of vegetables and often pie or perhaps cake or cookies for dessert. Christmas of course was extra special and preceded by many dreams as well as much secret activity to prepare the homemade gifts which we exchanged with each other. The aunts in Minnesota (Mother's side) and Illinois (Dad's first wife's family) usually sent bought presents (often books and games), invariably a collection of hard candies, and even more appealing, candied fruits. When the Christmas season was over the remaining candies were divided among us children. Each one got his or her share, either to be put away and saved as long as possible, or devoured immediately - depending upon the personality of the recipient.

Mom and Aunt Valesca sometimes made clothes for our presents. Two things Valesca gave me I still remember fondly - one a green silk dress, the back of the blouse finished with white cotton for want of enough material. Nothing that could not be amended by the jacket she made! The front of the blouse had horizontal pleats, and I did love that dress even though the fitting almost gave me a fit. When a dress in the making was being tried on I invariably thought I would suffocate before I was released. The other gift I remember was a delightful scrapbook, full of wonderful pictures and verses - something which is still somewhere squirreled away among my treasures. The boys at some point got skis - I am not sure what else. We got a sled, and several times I received dolls even though our folks had very little money to spend on anything other than necessities. The only really major disappointment I can remember was the year I wanted a doll buggy - a nice round wicker one like

I saw pictured in the Sears Roebuck catalog. I got a doll buggy, but it was a skinny, angular version, equipped with what I think must have been an oil-cloth seat and canopy. When I got older and realized how hard it was for my parents to make ends meet I fervently hoped that my disappointment had not been evident. I remember that I often yearned for the full page Christmas stocking crammed with gifts and goodies also displayed in the "wish book". When I got old enough to read the fine print I discovered that giant Christmas stocking was twelve inches high. So much for childish dreams and expectations!!

Christmas Eve was our big night. With relatives gathered and dinner finished, Dad (and the boys when old enough) repaired to the barn to milk the cows while the "womenfolk" did the dishes and the kids waited impatiently for "the action" to begin. Milking was not the end of the wait - the milk still had to be run through the separator. Then we could go into the living room, light the Christmas candles on the tree, with Dad standing by to provide fire safety, hear the Christmas story read, sing carols and open our gifts. The tree was normally cut in the nearby pine hills, except for the year we substituted a plum tree from the yard because Dad was not able to harvest one with needles. I still think a tree is not quite a Christmas tree unless there are flickering candles on it, but just as safety precautions have made Fourth of July fireworks all but obsolete for home use, so live candles on Christmas trees are pretty much a thing of the past.

Christmas day was the occasion for another big meal, and the initiation of whatever new games, toys and gadgets we had received. For a few days thereafter the remnants of the goodies were there for the taking - and maybe sharing with neighbors who dropped in to join us in some Christmas cheer.

My father was of German Swiss extraction, but I do not recall we ever had any dishes related to his childhood or ethnic background. However in addition to the usual cookies, cakes and breads common to all American households my mother's Norwegian heritage was drawn on rather heavily, particularly at Christmas. Sot Suppe (sweet soup) we had quite often, including sometimes at Christmas. It was a bit like compote with prunes, raisins, and possibly other fruits cooked together with rice or tapioca and served hot. Sometimes we had lutefisk (lye fish) at Christmas. This was cod soaked in lye. In preparation it was "de-lyed" by soaking in water, then cooked (gently because the texture became almost like jelly) and eaten with melted butter and for those who liked it that way, with vinegar. This was no doubt a product of Norway, and I have no idea how we were able to get it. There certainly were not many Norwegians living in Powder River County; probably the shopkeepers were able to get it from Miles City at the request of the locals. Some members of the family, perhaps notably my half-siblings who were German Swiss and Irish were never very fond of this dish.

Other Norwegian fare included in our Christmas menus were: rommegrot a flour and milk pudding eaten with cinnamon and sugar. This was a poor relative of the much richer flotegrod (Cream Porridge) which was made of pure cream heated slowly until the drawn butter separated in pools and puddles. This Norwegian dish was traditionally eaten with lingonberries, a Norwegian fruit something like tiny cranberries. I think I first tasted it when I went to college in the very Scandinavian town of Decorah, Iowa. Actually we called our poor man's version flotegrod and the rich relative rommegrot - but who can argue with a Scandinavian cookbook?

Fattigmand bakkels (poor man's cookies) were made from egg dough, rolled thin and cut in a diamond shape with a slit in the center. When fried in deep fat (lard in our home) they would curl, puff and bubble and especially if dusted with sugar provided a pleasing crunchy morsel. Smor kranser (butter wreaths) were rich cookies something like scotch breads. Occasionally we had Berliner kranser (Berlin wreaths) made with many eggs and shaped into script type "e's" before baking. Julekage or julebrod (Christmas bread) was filled with raisins and, if available, candied fruit. After I got old enough to try my hand at baking I sometimes made potato lefse which we kids called dishrags. These were made of flour and potato dough, rolled thin to the size of small dinner plates and "baked" one by one on a griddle or skillet, until they developed small brown blotches. They could be eaten spread with butter and rolled up like a jelly roll, or buttered, sprinkled with sugar and rolled, or if you were a true Norwegian, filled with lutefisk.

Many Norwegian specialties seem designed to be labor intensive including many varieties I learned to make as an adult: Sand bakkels (sand tarts) which are pressed like thin shells into the small tins in which they are baked; krum kake (crumb cake) made individually in an iron something like a waffle iron, (but with much shallower indentations), then rolled around a test tube or wooden rod or cone. These, called "crispy nothings" by a friend of mine, shatter if you look at them crosseyed. Rosettes are made from a batter and fried in deep fat. The rosette iron has one or two metal forms which are dipped into batter, then lowered into the fat. When finished the rosettes may be dusted with powdered or granulated sugar, and I guess might be called "crispy somethings". Kringler are somewhere between a bread and a cookie. Like Berliner kranser pieces of dough are rolled into short ropes and formed into script "e's" before baking.

Fourth of July was a community celebration. As far as I remember there were always festivities in Broadus, and we always attended. Sometimes the events included games and contests, and possibly a parade. Sometimes barbecued pig and other goodies were provided by the merchants and supplemented the picnic lunches we brought from home. This was a great time for the kids, and no doubt also for the grownups as people gathered from a radius of perhaps fifteen to twenty miles to meet, greet, play and visit with friends and relatives. For the young people I guess it was also a great opportunity to cast about for that special person who sometimes ended up being one's life partner.

We invariably had fireworks at home - mostly sparklers, firecrackers, and rockets. I suppose there may have been accidents, but they must have been few and far between for I remember none; the safety concerns of recent years had not yet put a stop to this beloved and thrilling way of celebrating our national independence. I am sure we gave little or no thought to the meaning of the day; but we did put a good deal of store by the chance to take our shovel full of live coals and translate them into the beauty of a sparkler brightening our small world or a rocket soaring into the darkness of the sky. I did sustain one small injury the effect of which is still visible today: during one of these annual soirees my hand was impaled by a paring knife bearing a live coal - and wielded by my next older sibling. In batting at it in self defense I managed to collect a trace of charcoal in the puncture.

In 1988 I re-visited Broadus for its Fourth of July celebration. There was a parade - quite good I thought - and I did see some old friends and neighbors. There may have been an afternoon rodeo. However by noon most of the crowd had melted away, probably in many cases to a celebration with their own family and friends. But the old community cohesion seemed to be lacking, and the memories of former days were bitter sweet.

With fewer people living on combined acreages, with (perhaps) a little greater level of affluence, and with greater mobility (virtually everyone now has a car) Independence Day celebrations are not limited to Broadus - one can easily go to Miles City, Belle Fourche, South Dakota, perhaps even Billings or Sheridan, Wyoming.

The year 1989 was the fiftieth anniversary of my high school graduation. and again I spent the Fourth in Broadus. It was also Montana's centennial. As a consequence of these two celebrations the town was jumping, and the programs excellent. The gorgeous weather, the hospitality of the townsfolk, returning classmates, the combined outdoor Sunday service of the three local churches (Catholic, Community and Lutheran) the outstanding local museum, the near-professional revue of Montana's one hundred year history made me realize that much of the old spirit remains. Though I have little contact anymore I am grateful for those who continue to make the community a vital force in spite of change. The misleading advertising done by the railroads in the early years, advertising meant to entice settlers to this "land of milk and honey" which in turn would ensure the survival of the magnates who owned the rails, no doubt led to many sad tales of failure; on the other hand there were some successes, and in spite of the struggle the dance goes on.with the hardy and the fortunate who are left. Even for those of us who did not stay, the frontier legacy - the self reliance, the ability to "make do" with little when it is necessary, is a legacy worth having.

The holidays I have just described were the icing on the cake; now we come to the meat and potatoes which after all are precious too, and provided the daily sustenance without which the icing would not have been possible or as deeply appreciated, and which made up the warp and woof of the homesteader's life. This daily life was the background pattern, the holidays the special designs which added brightness to the entire motif.

Daily work, and the chores which keep every farmer on a short tether occupied most of our time. Sometimes the work was difficult, tiresome, and worrying. The young do not spend much time on the worrying; that seems to be the job of parents. But we kids sometimes appreciated tiresome, and perhaps absorbed more than we ever voiced or realized the uncertainty and precariousness of farm life - especially farm life in Montana. At any rate, none of us kids stayed; we all moved on. I am not sure if this was intentional; I think in the case of the boys it was. They probably felt there were better, easier? opportunities elsewhere. Philip from high school age knew he wanted to be a doctor. That automatically took him on a detour from Montana. Frank was always interested in mechanics,and when he had a chance to stay with relatives in Chicago and take airplane mechanics he jumped at the chance. His work led him to Sikeston, Missouri, then to East St. Louis where he met and married

Julie Rojaz. settling shortly after in Belleville where he and Julie raised their family.

My older sisters married and after short stints on farm and ranch "went west" - Madeline and Jess to Deer Lodge where he became a guard at the Montana state penetentiary, Margaret and Art to Salmon, Idaho where the land held them until the war. Both families moved on during war time - Madeline and her family to Chicago where they lived with her mother's relatives and Jess worked in a war plant; Margaret and her family first to the Oregon coast where Art worked in a shipyard (also war related) until the war ended; then he moved on and settled in Klamath Falls, Oregon where he became an electrician. Madeline and Jess, after the war, also went to Klamath Falls where Jess did custodial work in the local conservation office until, after his retirement, they moved to California to be near their three daughters.

For my part, I think the decision not to remain in Montana was more or less accidental. Philip and I had the opportunity to go to college. We chose Luther College in Decorah, Iowa primarily because my mother was Lutheran and one of her forebears in Norway had set up a legacy for relatives which required American recipients to go out of state for their higher education.

The happenstance of my going there, settling on a degree in biology, being influenced by my biology professor to get a Master's degree and then during wartime having an opportunity to teach at Waldorf

College in Forest City, Iowa was just that - it happened, and was not planned.

To return to the "meat and potatoes" of our life in Montana: during our work week we did not wander far afield except for school and occasionally to accompany our parents to Broadus on a shopping trip. Evenings were often spent, especially in winter and after the chores were done, in reading, playing board games, doing crafts, or listening to Mom read us stories. There were times when we ventured forth in sleigh or lumber wagon, even at night, for a winter event bundled against the cold and with hot irons at our feet. This might either be a visit to a neighbor's, or a dance or party. During the day it would likely be a Sunday when we might go for dinner to a neighbor's, or in turn they might come to our place - visits often unannounced.

There were community dances, but as the years passed these became less frequent as family affairs. My brothers and sisters (mainly the three older ones) as they became high school age and beyond went greater distances to dances with their peers. By the time Philip and I were old enough to participate (other than in high school events) there were not many young people in our community and most of our social life during the school year centered around whatever was happening at Broadus High School. During high school your grandfather played basketball and took part in field events.

I sang in the glee club. As a family we usually attended functions at the school such as games and plays, and I recall being in one school production: I had one line in "Who's Crazy Now?" and was terrified I would get rattled and forget it. I also recall at least one show in which we modeled old fashioned clothes. Even before attending high school I remember occasional times when we went to Broadus to attend a chautauqua or other entertainment. In later years there was a movie theater in Broadus, but I do not remember attending more than one or two movies there.

After I was old enough to remember, our faithful "skypilot" who lived with his family near Coalwood, came about once a month to our little country school to preach. On Sundays when he did not come, we always had our own services at home, with Bible reading, songs and prayer. After we got our pump organ and learned to play there would be what passed for an accompaniment. During summers we either had Bible vacation school at the Durst school, or sometimes the minister would take us younger children to stay in his home and attend vacation school in Coalwood.

Early on there was a Catholic church in Broadus, and later a community church, but we never attended there. The Lutheran church was organized years later.

Through our grade school years there was a good deal of social interaction in the community. Besides dances, and neighbors' visits there were neighborhood baseball games almost every Sunday in summer. Those who came to these were mostly our nearest neighbors - William Rule, the Watters family, Amsden's, the Ambuel's. Sunday visits either to or from friends and family were often all day affairs. Sometimes there were picnics in the pine hills. Often there were large summer gatherings, usually picnics with crowds of up to sixty or seventy people present.

In retrospect it is amazing to me how rich a childhood and youth we had, how wholesome the fabric of the community in spite of the extremes of weather, the relative isolation, the economic difficulties, the diversity in ethnic and social background; it is also amazing to me how well our parents did in providing a good home, good values, the little things that make life rich, in spite of the constant struggle just to provide the physical necessities of life. Did we realize it then? Probably not, but realizing it now makes me very grateful and also makes me wish all children could be so blessed.

Aunt Louise

LETTERS VIA CHINOOK

To My Grandchildren
Laura, Brian, David, Philip

CHILDHOOD MEMORIES: A Day in the Life of a Schoolboy on a Montana Farm

A day in the life of a farm boy growing up in Eastern Montana was profoundly influenced by two facts: the distances between neighbors is measured in miles, not in blocks, and work on the farm is never done.

CHORES - CHORES - CHORES.
WORK - WORK - WORK

JUST REMEMBER - ALL WORK AND NO PLAY MAKES JIM A DULL BOY!

When I was growing up in Montana our closest neighbors were about a half mile from our house, and our closest neighbor with children in the home was two miles distant. One did not easily "drop in" for an after school chat with one's playmates.

From an early age (probably four or five years) we were expected to help with chores. Work around the farm can be thought of as "Big Work" or "chores". Big Work includes such things as plowing the fields, cutting and stacking the hay, threshing, butchering pigs or steers, canning vegetables and fruit, washing and ironing clothes. Chores are typically things that must be done every day of the year, summer and winter, rain or shine so that daily life can go on. There is some work that sort of falls between chores and Big Jobs - like milking the cows. Not every farm in Montana had milk cows, but in our case milking eight to ten cows morning and evening every day turns out to be a really Big Job. Preparing meals three times a day every day is obviously a Big Job, but an even bigger job is the work of canning done in a few short weeks when the garden is producing far more than we can eat in that short a time. In general canning would not be thought of as a chore, but preparing breakfast on a Wednesday morning might be thought of as a chore for the teenage girl or boy.

So what are some of the more typical chores?

Filling the woodbox in the kitchen with firewood

Filling the coal bucket in the kitchen and by the bedroom stoves

Filling the reservoir of the stove with clean water from the well

Gathering eggs; feeding the chickens

Milking the cows; feeding the calves

Fetching water

Splitting wood for the kitchen stove

Carrying coal from the shed to the house

Sawing and chopping wood for the stoves

Hoeing weeds from the garden

Washing vegetables and potatoes to clean for food

Separating cream from the milk with the cream separator

Threshing time was always a high point of the year. It ranked with Christmas and the Fourth of July. For a non-holiday to have competed with these two major holidays is no small achievement.

What is it with threshing time?

The end of the year

Time to measure your success as a farmer and

Put to rest all those worries about spring frost, drought, grasshoppers, Mormon crickets, hail storms...

But from the child's standpoint these are not the major reasons for celebration. What it is is...

The buzz of activity

Strangers on the farmstead

The excitement of seeing all the individual tasks of the threshing crew merge into a smooth running operation with the result being a pile of wheat, barley or oats in one of our granaries.

It really is fascinating to observe: for days and even weeks prior to threshing day the ripened grain has been cut by a binder, tied in bundles, and stacked in shocks with the grains of the wheat pointing skyward. On the day of threshing these bundles of wheat must be stacked on hay wagons as they are picked up from the field, carried to the threshing machine, and pitched from the hay wagons into the gaping mouth of the machine.

Since the object of the endeavor is to get the kernels of grain separated from the straw and to do it with as little wasted effort as possible it takes a bit of estimating. How many hay wagons - usually made up of two horses to pull the wagon, two men to drive the team and pitch the bundles of grain from the shocks to the hay wagon then drive the wagon to the threshing machine and pitch the bundles of grain into its mouth. How long will it take to finish the job at the Ambuel farm so that the next farmer can be alerted to be ready for the threshing crew?

While the men and boys are busy with the threshing job the women and girls of the Ambuel ranch are equally busy preparing and serving the food.

Threshing time demands an extra effort from the food crew beginning with the basics of the farm diet: meat, potatoes, vegetables and bread, and ending with dessert - usually cake, cookies and pie and coffee.

IT IS A DAY TO BE REMEMBERED!!

That is all for now...Until next time

Best wishes

Be good

Keep the peace

Grandpa

Letters
Via Chinook

To My Grandchildren
Laura, Brian, David, Philip

Welcome to the World of the Weird!!

The Wild Wind of the West brings you another Silly Symphony. A Silly Symphony is a whimsical ditty - a fun rhyme that you can say or sing. It's meaning is obscure and only understood by spirits and elves. Let your imagination be your guide.

OH WHAT ARE YOU GOING TO DO?

Oh, what are you going to do
when the rooster won't crow in the morning?
Oh what are you going to do
when the cock won't crow?
What are you going to do
when the turkey won't gobble
and the duck won't quack

OH

What will you do?
Will you wiggle your toes? Will you giggle?

OR

twitch your nose?

It may be too late
to correct your fate
when the rooster
won't crow in the morning!

A CHICKADEE IS NOT A TREE

A chickadee is not a tree....
As anyone can plainly see, a chickadee is not a tree.
A cat may be a kitten but a cap is not a mitten.
An acorn may become a tree (if it is not eaten first)
An egg is not a chicken and a mouse is not a mitten.
Just remember girls and boys
An egg is not a chicken and a mouse is not a mitten.
In this topsy turvy world
East may be West and North may be South

but

A chickadee is NOT a tree!

That is all for now...Until next time

Best wishes
Be good
Keep the peace

Grandpa

Letters Via Chinook

To My Grandchildren
Laura, Brian, David, Philip

Odds, Ends and Ideas

There comes a time in the telling of any story when one must "clear the deck", so to speak, thus clearing up some of those fuzzy edges. This is one of those times.

One of my favorite sayings from frontier America is "There is more than one way to skin a cat".

NOW
I have never skinned a cat
I have never seen anyone skin a cat
I don't know why I would want to
see anyone skin a cat

This is a catchy phrase, but it also means there is more than one way to do something.

****

A smashed egg does not a chicken make, but it sure helps your prize winning cake.

A rooster is a cock when it crows the sun awake.

Eggs are eggs; acorns are acorns; trees are trees and twine ties the threesome together.

Magic builds us up, magic tears us down, but just remember girls and boys .....

Some thought the world was round BUT
the wise men knew it was flat AND
to prove their point they stretched the heretics
on the rack or burned them at the stake.

****

A stitch in time saves nine. I wonder who did the study to prove this statement. Why not a timely stitch saves ten or twenty or one hundred? Don't be silly young man. Everyone knows it is nine! A little work now saves much work next year.

****

Conversation overheard at a Sunday picnic between two middle aged mothers:

Mrs. A - "I see you are expecting".

Mrs. B - "Yes, this will be number nine".

Mrs. A. -"When are you planning to stop?"

Mrs. B. -"Oh, I don't know! It seems a body ought to have at least a dozen"

****

Have you ever noticed how some words are acceptable in polite society and other words that mean about the same are not, or at least are sort of relegated to the barnyard? For example, in my high school days it was common for us to say that a friend or foe had a lot of guts, meaning he had a lot of courage and was a tough opponent. When I entered Luther College I was impressed by some of the older boys who introduced me to the much more elegant term "intestinal fortitude".

Take another term: "shit". During my boyhood days we used "shit" in the barnyard, and "manure" if we were talking to the family around the dinner table. It seemed very inappropriate for me to use the term "shit" at the kitchen table. Many years later when there had been a big change in the common language used I came into my office just in time to hear my secretary (a young woman twenty three years old) use the term when talking to her cohorts. When she saw me she was obviously embarrassed and despite years of contact with the world, I found the use of the word in that context to be a distinctly uncomfortable experience. Now don't get me wrong. I am in favor of polite conversation and civilized discussions. I see no advantage in using barnyard language in trying to promote serious discussion of important issues. It seems to me that you should be aware of how certain words have come to carry extra meaning which will only tend to confuse the issue.

Take the word "shit". Would you feel more comfortable if I said "manure"? Consider the word "bitchy". One of my old dictionaries defines this as a female member of the canine family. How did a loving, over protective mother get associated with this derogatory phrase?

That is all for now...Until next time
Best wishes
Be good
Keep the peace

Grandpa

Letters Via Chinook

To My Grandchildren

Laura, Brian, David, Philip

Detour With Aunt Louise in Collaboration with Grandpa and Uncle Jack: The Land, The Farm, and Farming Practices

Southeastern Montana is traversed by the Powder River, a tributary of the Missouri which in turn is a tributary of the Mississippi. It is a shallow river, often almost dry, with stretches of cottonwoods lining its banks. The country through which it passes is short grass prairie, flat as the eye can see in some places, in others accented by pine hills, buttes, gullies, draws and coulees. Wild plum, chokecherry, buffalo berry and other small trees and bushes grow, mostly along the coulees, and sweet scented wild roses lend their beauty to any suitable spot. Liberally dotting the prairie are spreading cactus (the kind with thick, flat, sections joined end to end) and woody, greyish sagebrush, some gnarled with age. Russian thistles grow up to three feet in diameter and are most evident when, breaking loose from their moorings, they roll across the landscape driven by strong Montana winds.

Among these larger plants are scores of smaller herbs, including many which produce showy flowers with the welcome spring rains.

Because of the scant rainfall (on average no more than ten to twelve inches per year) there has been no opportunity for the accumulation of the deep, rich loam typical of the tall grass prairie to the east. In Iowa, Indiana, Ohio, Southern Minnesota, and Wisconsin, and even the eastern portion of the Dakotas, rainfall was sufficent so that grasses grew abundantly; year by year as the grasses died and decayed they formed the humus that makes these soils so fertile. No such fertile loam built up in southeastern Montana. While the scant rainfall meant there was little leaching of soil nutrients, the soil lacks the characteristics of good, deep loam. There is almost never enough rain, and homesteaders all too often had to suffer through prolonged periods of drought; severe droughts could sometimes stretch from one year to the next.

The soil (classed as deep silt loam and fine sandy loam according to the U.S. Department of Agriculture Soil Conservation Service general soil map) is, because of its low humus content, light in color and not overly productive. However given sufficient rain, crop yields can be quite high - rarely up to 60 bushels of wheat per acre. In some places there were areas of heavy clay (gumbo) which after heavy rains, could hopelessly mire a car. Patches of light gumbo on our farm did not seriously interfere with cultivation. So far as I know, we never used commercial fertilizers; however we did use both green and barnyard manure.

Because of climatic and weather conditions, Montana is less suited to farming than to grazing. However in the more favorable western portion of the state a number of farms sprang up, partly in response to the needs of prospectors and settlers farther to the west and partly due to the development of the railroads and their opening of Montana lands for settlement. Wheat was grown over large acreages principally in the central Montana plains where irrigation was possible.

In some parts of Montana there were large cattle, and sheep ranches. One occasionally heard rumors of conflicts between sheep and cattle men who threatened each others' turf, mostly carved out of the open range. It was claimed that sheep damage the prairie because they graze too close; due to the light rainfall roots are shallow and with close grazing the grass is damaged or destroyed.

Though sometimes thought of as ranches, most of the holdings in the vicinity of Broadus (the seat of Powder River County) were farms - relatively small acreages, most originally acquired by homesteading. In the early 1900s the government was still giving away land to citizens who were willing to "prove up" a claim by building a cabin and living on the property for a certain number of years (three at the time our parents arrived). The claims at that time were a half section (320 acres) and most people acquired more land by purchase This was necessary since dry land farming requires a larger acreage than in regions with more abundant rainfall or where irrigation is possible. Both our mother and father homesteaded in the area, and though their holdings were not adjacent, at a later date our mother's property was exchanged for a parcel which adjoined our land. In addition our parents acquired land from Jack East, a homesteader who moved on for one reason or another. For many, homesteading must have been a nightmare, or at the very least a challenge. The rosy pictures painted by promoters, including railroad owners who sought to encourage settlers and thereby ensure their own success, were rarely if ever borne out in fact.

In addition to the land we owned our father leased the school section which lay directly to the east. Our property must have eventually incorporated 1000 acres, since when my mother sold the farm in 1945 she received $5000 - five dollars per acre. Several years later we were told the buyer resold for fifteen dollars per acre.

The only source of water for crops was whatever precipitation the weather blessed us with. Field irrigation was not common, although sometimes dikes were built to divert the spring rains from creeks to fields. For stock and household use, people depended on wells. There was a small spring on our property some distance from the house. It was never really developed, although our father fenced it to prevent trampling by the animals and in the summer it provided drinking water for our cattle. As I remember, it also provided a habitat for dragon flies, frogs and tadpoles as well as other creatures which would normally find the prairie uninviting.

Our first well was shallow, the water hard, and available only by use of a hand pump. When I was perhaps six or seven our father hired a well driller who drilled a deeper well. Since it was equipped with a windmill, and Montana is quite windy, the stock tank was kept filled and water was available for the nearby fruit trees. The fruit trees and your grandpa's flowers were the only lucky recipients of water delivered directly to them. Our farming was strictly dry land farming. Our uncle, John Gaar, who lived three miles east of us had on his property an artesian (flowing) well, no doubt the envy of many of his neighbors. During our childhood our father dug a fairly good sized reservoir, probably for swimming or other recreational purposes. The soil there was apparently unsuitable and it never held sufficient water to live up to the name "reservoir". Its main function in my mind was to provide the polliwogs I loved to catch in the spring, nurture in quart jars and watch as they grew fat and sassy.

Most of our rains fell in the spring. Sometimes these were torrential and filled the little gullies and creeks to overflowing. Frequently they were accompanied by deafening thunderclaps and blinding lightning. One such thunderclap was so loud it clearly must have been caused by a lightning strike very close at hand. Sure enough, we found a neat furrow stripped the length of two of our clothesline posts from top to bottom. Apparently the lightning had struck the center of the wire, traveled in both directions and grounded itself through the posts.

The spring rains brought out the prairie flowers and if we were lucky provided the good start necessary for a favorable harvest. By the end of June most of our rains were over. There might of course be storms later in the summer, but often they were dry storms. The rolling thunder and flashing lightning would prove to be only bluster. Thor must not have been serious, merely swinging his hammer for fun. By late June or early July the grass was dry and brown - quite a contrast to the lush green still visible in September in the midwest. This dry grass, however, was a boon to cattle (and other grazing animals), for it "cured on the ground" and provided good grazing throughout the winter as long as the animals could reach it.

Winter snows usually began by November and lasted through February or more likely March. On occasion heavy snowstorms would arrive as late as May. Blizzards were particularly treacherous snowstorms with blinding snow whipped by the prairie winds. There were stories of blizzards so bad one could not "see his hand in front of his face"; on occasion one heard tales of people freezing to death within feet of their houses. Our Dad always told us if a blizzard came up while we were on horseback to "give the horse its head" and it would likely take us home.

The Chinook winds your Grandpa has already told you about and for which these letters are named would sometimes begin their banishment of winter only to be beaten back by an icy blast from the north and a new blanket of snow. Total snowfall was often quite considerable, deep enough to cover the fence running across the hill in the back pasture, and no doubt gave an assist to the spring rains in providing much needed soil moisture. Our entire farm including Dad's homestead and the lands purchased or exchanged amounted to about a thousand acres. At one time in the '60s there was a flurry of activity in oil speculation. At that time we received lease money of one dollar per acre from the oil company for exploration rights. There were producing wells north of Broadus (at Glendive near Miles City) and some were developed in Powder River County. Our total annual lease money at one time was around $700, so evidently we did not own mineral rights to all our land. The mineral rights still remain with the Ambuels even though the land was sold; however my mother in her deed to the buyer in 1945 included a portion of any oil revenue should producing wells ever be drilled.

Most of the farming in the area of Powder River County where we lived was mixed farming. By the time my parents settled there, the land was no longer open range; homesteaders fenced their properties. The railroads ran some distance north of us, and the more fertile lands were farther west. There were none of the huge ranches typical of some parts of Montana; most homesteaders owned relatively small acreages. All of this no doubt contributed to the diversification typical of these farms. Another factor in our case may have been that our father had farmed in Illinois in the St. Louis area and was no doubt more familiar with that type of farming.

Pastures, house and outbuildings took up about half our land. The remainder was under cultivation. Spring plowing was done by using a team of two horses. In later years some neighbors acquired tractors; however our farming never became mechanized. After plowing, the clods were broken up by discing and the harrow was used to further prepare the soil. During the growing season corn, which was our only open growing crop was cultivated to remove the weeds between the rows and to break up the surface so as to conserve soil moisture. The kids and Mom also sometimes "cultivated" closer to the plants by hoeing - a most unwelcome job especially when the sun was boiling hot, sometimes up to 110 degrees in the shade.

Our grain crops were corn, wheat, oats, and sometimes barley. Alfalfa and yellow sweet clover were raised for hay; during some of the dry years Russian thistles were harvested instead of or in addition to forage crops. A few years our alfalfa crop was good enough so that we had alfalfa seed for sale. Corn was planted by drilling, the smaller grains were broadcast. After spring planting the summer work consisted of cultivating, cutting hay, keeping up with the barnyard chores, and the garden which, along with the meat and milk from our farm animals, provided much of our year round sustenance. Summer was also the time when wood and coal was stockpiled for winter, fences were mended and other repairs and general upkeep was done.

We generally planted spring wheat, though one or two years we planted a crop of winter wheat. Summer fallowing was done to a small extent; perhaps our cultivated acreage was not sufficient to practice on a larger scale. To my knowledge there was little if any rotation practiced. Cultivation was the main method used to conserve soil moisture and control weeds. I do not recall that we ever used insecticides except to discourage potato bugs. Grasshoppers were a frequent problem, but there was not much that could be done about them. Some farmers may have used poisoning programs, but that was not done on our farm. There was also no way for us to control Mormon crickets which invaded one season and devoured virtually everything in sight - other than the garden which was protected by "boot patrol".

Water erosion was never a problem on our farm. Though the sometimes torrential spring rains might cause some road washouts, damage to the land and the fields was rarely if ever significant. Our fields were quite flat, so there was little chance of damaging runoff, and the pasture hills where the soil had never been broken had good tough sod to slow and hold the runoff. Cultivated land was of course open to erosion by wind, and Montana is a windy state. There was probably more soil lost by wind erosion than we realized or than was readily evident; during some of the drought years dust storms were common and almost blinding at times.

Because windows did not fit tight, it was necessary to plug the cracks with rags during some of the worst dust storms in order to keep the indoors relatively dust free. Few people used windbreaks, perhaps because it is not easy to raise trees in Montana.

Fall brought with it the work of cutting and shocking the corn (or picking the ears if the stalks were to be left in the field), shelling the corn, cutting, binding, and shocking the wheat and other grains, cutting and stacking hay, and threshing. Some farmers, though not the Ambuels, in later years had silos in which shredded cornstalks were stored and after fermentation became silage to supplement the hay and grains used to feed the livestock.

In the early years fall brought threshing crews which traveled from farm to farm, hired by each farmer to thresh his grain for storage or sale. Later, my father and two neighbors jointly owned a threshing machine. Soon after that association was dissolved combines took the place of threshing machines. Since combines cut and thresh the grain almost as a single operation, large threshing crews were no longer needed and the fun and camaraderie of threshing time, admittedly along with a lot of hard work, were no more.

Autumn was also the time for melons to be stored in the granary, potatoes dug and put in the cellar, for family expeditions to pick chokecherries and plums for canning, and garden produce to be harvested. In our garden we grew most kinds of vegetables: lettuce, radishes, cabbage, tomatoes, beets, peas, beans, swiss chard, spinach, onions, kohl rabi, turnips, rutabagas, carrots, squash, and sweet corn - usually in plentiful amount. Our winesap and crabapple trees provided us with fruit, along with currants, strawberries and raspberries (mostly eaten during the summer), and husk tomatoes and ground cherries which grew on bushes in the garden. Early maturing vegetables, such as peas and beans had already been picked, snapped and canned during the summer, but most vegetables and fruit had to be preserved or otherwise prepared for storage in the fall. We never had facilities for freezing or drying, so fruits or vegetables which would not keep in the cellar had to be canned.

Carrots were buried in sand in the cellar; potatoes, onions and other root vegetables put down in open bins, except for beets which were usually canned. Cabbage was thinly sliced and put to ferment into sauerkraut in large stone crocks behind the kitchen stove. Tomatoes were skinned and usually canned by the hot pack method. Any vegetables low in acid (peas, beans, corn,) were preserved by the cold pack method - i.e. cleaned, blanched and packed into jars which were then put into our old beat up copper boiler (used on washday to boil the clothes), and put on the kitchen range to process for hours. When sweet corn was ready to harvest for canning Dad performed one of his few household tasks: cutting the corn from the cob.

A number of fruits were also canned. Wild plums were made into sauce; chokecherries were canned as sauce or juice for syrup and jelly. Apple juice from our crabapple trees was put up to be made into jelly at some later time. Husk tomatoes with lemon slices added were put up as sauce. This was one of your Grandpa's favorites, and he seemed never to tire of it packed in old cold cream jars and tucked into his lunchbox. It was the rare year that we did not buy a crate or two of peaches, (one of the few foods we purchased) some to be eaten fresh, but most to be canned for the winter. Perhaps unique was our preparation of crabapples for sauce. Our yellow crabs could reach the size of cherry tomatoes; the red crabs, however, rarely became bigger than large marbles. These lilliputian fruits were quartered, cored and canned. Can you imagine a modern teenager assigned a job like that?!

Besides raising a variety of crops and garden produce the farm also supported a variety of animals: horses, cattle, pigs, chickens, turkeys (one year), guinea hens (a couple of years), a dog, and cats. We never had sheep. Most of our childhood years we had three saddle horses - Chip, our old faithful pony who carried us to school; Sam, and Alberta - gifts of Mr. Waltz to our older sisters, Madeline and Margaret. We also had at least two teams of work horses.

Generally eight to ten cows were milked morning and night, and our entire herd was probably seldom more than fifteen or twenty; the steers provided the beef for our table and some were sold for cash at the end of the summer. Occasionally we had a bull, but usually calves were sired by bulls from other herds. During the depression of the 1930's the government's attempt to shore up farm prices led to the slaughter of many cattle - including some of ours - which their owners did not have enough feed to maintain over winter.

Besides the milk, cream, butter and buttermilk used by the family, cream was sold for extra cash. Cream was added daily to the large steel cream cans kept in the cellar. Some of that was appropriated for topping breakfast pancakes, but there was a good deal left for Dad to transport to Broadus once a week. From there it was sent to a creamery in Miles City, ninety miles away. Our first butter churn was a tall stoneware crock with a pole attached to a butter paddle. When the paddle was raised and lowered enough times, one could eventually churn butter out of the rich cream separated morning and night as the whole milk was run through the separator. I seem to remember our mother telling that sometimes our dad churned and he would get so impatient he would dance the churn around the floor. While I was still small we got a barrel churn - a big improvement on the original. To churn butter in that, one sat on a chair and turned a crank. It probably held at least ten gallons and the job was still tedious - but better than before. After we got that churn, and could churn faster and more efficiently Dad sometimes sold butter as well as cream and meat. I recall that he had a one pound butter mold into which he would put butter paper (a special wrapping paper), add a big dollop of butter with a butter paddle, and close the mold. I remember my mother admiring the skill with which he could slap the butter into the mold - just the right amount, just the right place for a perfect result. Cheese we never made, other than cottage cheese.

Perhaps ten or fifteen pigs were raised for butchering and for sale in the fall. They were kept in a pigpen somewhere in the barnyard. They foraged for themselves, as well as receiving oats, some milk and kitchen scraps and slops. During one or two really bad years, they were fed cactus cooked in a big cooker.

The chicken coop housed perhaps twenty hens and several roosters. Brooding hens often would steal away in the spring to a distant hideout to lay the eggs that they would try to hatch in secret. Eggs were gathered once a day and the girls at least found this a bit of a challenge, especially during brooding when the hen with her maternal instincts at the ready was like as not to give the gatherer a peck. The chickens got much of their feed by scratching for themselves, but this was supplemented with wheat.

We usually had plenty of eggs and the chickens provided a quick and handy source of meat for our table. Extra eggs were peddled in Broadus - for five cents a dozen. One of the oft told family anecdotes was the story of either your Grandpa or your Uncle Frank who had the job of watering the chickens. The little chickens were given water in mason jar caps so as to be more accessible to them. Whoever was responsible for the chore, when asked why he covered the jar caps said he wanted to keep the big chickens from drinking the little chicks' water. Innocence or guile?? The attempt to raise turkeys was a fiasco. The birds seemed to have constant health problems, and the experiment lasted for only one year.

Steers and pigs were not butchered until freezing weather arrived. Chickens could be killed for home or company at any season of the year, since they would be used at once. Several pigs and a steer were usually butchered each fall. For extra cash Dad peddled meat door to door in Broadus; for this he got the princely sum of ten cents a pound! Of course Cracker Jacks (a favorite treat for the small fry) at that time cost only five cents, so he could buy two boxes of Cracker Jacks for a pound of meat. Beef steaks were favorite fare at butchering time, and some was put down in lard for winter use. Mom canned much of the beef as beef stew - delicious as were most of her meats. Some she put up as meatballs. The cellar was always plentifully stocked by winter's advent, even in years when drought or insects robbed us of our usual supply of vegetables and fruit.

Hams and bacons were smoked in the smokehouse and also provided winter fare. One household task Dad performed on cold winter evenings, often while Mother read from a story book, was cleaning pigs heads for head cheese (some call it scrapple), and pigs feet for the yummy pickled pigs feet which was one of my favorite foods. The old saying "you can use all of a pig except its squeal" was certainly true in our household. Pork loin was sometimes canned. In addition to the pigs we used for food, your Grandpa raised pigs for the fair. These were usually sold following the fair and the awarding of prizes. Your Uncle Frank raised corn instead of pigs for the fair, and I baked cookies and made aprons.

There was an effort to shelter the animals when the weather was very bad, though we certainly did not have enough barn space for all our animals even in bitter winter weather. If they were outside there were sheds, haystacks and the farm buildings to give them some protection. We had both a horse barn and a cowbarn, each with an adjacent corral. I recall at times the horses being in the barn when they were not at work or out to pasture. Since the grass matured on the ground the animals could graze in the pastures late in the season provided there was not too much snow. They were fed oats and when necessary, in winter and if the pasture grasses were insufficient, they were also given hay.

In the cowbarn there were stanchions for the cows while they were being milked. Sometimes they were left in the barn overnight. Even in very cold weather the other cattle were out of doors. While being milked the cows were fed hay, and whenever pasture grasses were inadequate or inaccessible they were given hay from the haystacks for daily feeding. You have already heard that in very bad drought years they sometimes had to be content with Russian thistle hay. Calves were weaned early and for a time received a share of the milking morning and night.

The Ambuel homestead began with a house and a barn, but as years passed it grew into a respectable and serviceable collection of buildings. The house consisted of a log kitchen and bedroom (the latter subdivided into two rooms) connected by a sod room. The kitchen was heated by a large iron range which was kept going with wood and coal through the daylight hours. Besides providing heat for the room, it served for cooking, canning, and heating of water for clothes washing. The big zinc washtub was also situated in front of this stove or by the one in the sod room for the Saturday night bath. During the week any personal washing up was done as a "spit bath" (a sponge bath) using a washbasin. Dad usually emptied the ashes and started the kitchen fire before he went out in the morning to milk the cows. At night the fire was allowed to go out, and it was not unusual of a winter morning to find ice in the water bucket and thick frost on the door hinges.

Off the kitchen on the east side was a summer kitchen, and on the west side was a "back room" which was a catch all for any household overflow. This room also contained the cellar door which opened to the stairs leading into the capacious cellar. In the cellar were the potato and carrot bins, shelves for canned goods, wall cupboards to keep milk, butter and cream in the winter, and even in the summer to store items not suitable for storage in the water tank in the well house. I do not now remember if perhaps the cellar also housed the coal bin.

When the cellar was dug, several feet under the surface, a trail was found - presumably an old buffalo trail. The mound covering the cellar was where our mother stood on summer days to wave a white towel and "yoo-hoo" the menfolks in from the field for dinner. ("Dinner" was always at noon; the night meal was "supper"). The roof, reminiscent in a ragged sort of way of Scandinavian buildings, was sodded, and grew a not very luxuriant crop of weeds.

The center room was built from sod slabs cut out of the topsoil, and stacked to form the walls. The slabs in our sod room were perhaps one and one half to two feet thick. Because of the tough grass roots binding the soil, these slabs of sod are remarkably strong and resilient. In addition they provide wonderful insulation, keeping out the cold in winter and the heat in summer. Our sod room was divided into a "sitting room" to the west, and a section to the east separated by portieres which served as our parents bedroom. There was also a trundle bed which was pulled out from under the double bed at night and which was used by the little kids. Later as the older children went away to high school the younger ones moved up into the "big kids" bedrooms - one of which was the room where the ridgepole broke. The sod room was unquestionably the most comfortable -particularly in frigid and torrid weather. Summer jobs like shelling peas, and winter activities such as reading at night were usually done in this room. This also was the site of both our sisters' marriages: Madeline's in June, under an arch of spirea, Margaret's in December under an arch of evergreen. This room was heated by a wood and coal stove, similar to a potbelly, but without the pot, which ensured that the room would be cozy day and night.

Between the sod room and the "front room" (the bedroom) was a very small connecting room. Two or three steps led up to the bedroom and on each side was a narrow "closet". The only other places we had to put away clothes were a makeshift closet along the wall of the farther bedroom, a wardrobe in our parents' room, and two big wooden boxes, one perhaps three by eight by four feet which sat in front of the kitchen window. Into this we tossed our outdoor clothes. The other, half again as large, was in our parent's bedroom. Montana homesteaders and their children, needless to say, were hardly clothes horses!

The "front bedroom" was occupied by not much other than a bed and dresser in each section, a stove in the front room, and the wall "closet" in the back - which in fact was only a long shelf supplied with hooks and a covering curtain. It was heated by a small "laundry" stove. That stove was tiny, but it packed a punch. Before bedtime the fire was started in this little stove, and within minutes both rooms (separated only by a partition) were toasty.

Other farm buildings were the outhouse (the "path"); the smokehouse (built of sod and one of my favorites for its smoky smell); the ice house (practically never used for ice), the well house (built around the old well and containing a wooden tank through which the water from the windmill ran to reach the stock tank). At one end of this tank a shallow section had been built to serve as a summer time cooler for melons, jars of milk and the root beer we sometimes made. Completing the outbuildings were the chicken house, (down the lane from the water tank and garden); the cow corral and cowbarn; the horse corral and horsebarn; the original log granary (its ridgepole extending out in front where carcasses of pigs and steers were suspended for butchering). When I last visited in 1988 this old granary was still standing and in relatively good condition. Most of the others buildings were either not visible at all, or were in a state of collapse. Two latecomers to our farmstead were the garage and the round metal granary, the latter being the only building not built by family labor.

Considering the time, effort and skill required to build and keep up these buildings, as well as attend to the thousand and one other responsibilities of a homestead, I think our parents and the other homesteaders were remarkable.

Ranchers frequently had hired men. At that time a dollar a day, meals and lodging (in the bunkhouse) seemed to be the going arrangement. Most farmers did not have hired help except for special projects and perhaps at harvest time. I do not recall full time hired men in our neighborhood, although one of our neighbors had a bunkhouse.

Perhaps that was for the overflow kids of the household, or perhaps they more frequently had hired help than most farmers.

I do not recall that we ever had hired help except for the threshing crews and the well drilling outfit. There were occasions when the neighbors exchanged help, particularly for special projects such as putting up a building. In the earliest days, Dad must have been responsible for nearly everything. There were times no doubt when our mother would be called from her household tasks to serve as an extra hand. Also Eli and Mike Severovic lived close by at that time. They were teenagers or preteens and were probably called on to help in minor ways. After the Ambuel boys got old enough, they provided the help Dad needed to run the farm - doing chores, milking cows, helping in the fields, running errands.

The little outside work I did was mostly garden work, especially weeding and picking fruit and vegetables, on occasion hoeing corn and sometimes serving as "gofer" at such times as butchering. The only time I tried to milk cows was after my father's death in 1940. I was not handy, and that assignment was soon withdrawn. Indoors I helped with preparing meals, baking (cookies, not bread - my mother did that), washing dishes (and the separator disks - ugh!), sweeping, dusting, mopping. These tasks were frequently interrupted by a hasty dash to read a few surreptitious lines from my current story book. My mother often preferred to work in the garden, so there were times when I was given the responsibility of doing the dishes and preparing meals. I well remember, since one of my sins was frequently oversalting the potatoes. Two other sins for which I got a lot of scolding were breaking dishes and burning cookies. My father had a cookie pan made which exactly fit the oven - at least two and a half feet square. When one burned a batch of cookies in that pan, one burned a lot of cookies.

Your Grandpa began college in 1937. Your Uncle Frank had already left for Idaho. In the spring of 1940, after your Grandpa's junior year and my freshman year at Luther College, our father (your great grandfather) died suddenly of perforated ulcers of the stomach. Our mother's brother, Willie, had come to Montana several years before to headquarter with us and carry on his work as a salesman. He also helped out on the farm since our father was not well. During the summers subsequent to Dad's death our Uncle Will was the mainstay for our mother, and your Grandpa also continued to help on the farm, during the summers. Following your Grandpa's graduation from college he spent a year teaching at his alma mater, Luther College in Decorah, Iowa. The following year he was accepted into the Naval Reserve and began his medical studies at the University of Chicago. After that he was not able to help at home. Two years later I completed Luther College, went on to a year of graduate study at the University of Michigan and began teaching at Waldorf College in Forest City, Iowa. In 1945, my second year of teaching, our

Mother sold the farm and moved to Forest City to live with me. After a generation the era of the Ambuel homesteaders was at an end.

The house was not used much after our mother left. The buyer of the Ambuel farm, Mr.Whitcher. may have lived there briefly or occasionally. The property was resold several years later and has since had other owners. For a time some of the land was used for cropland by Donald Manker, who was then living on the old Rule place a couple of miles away. At present the land is owned by Phyllis and Bernard (Mike) Landa who bought the Waltz property on Powder River. They run cattle; for that more land is needed than for farming. The old ways of life in the neighborhood have pretty much vanished. Of the old neighbors only two I know of are still on the original family farms: Elmer Watters a few miles north of our place and Carl Ullrich three or four miles south and east. Another place on the fringe of our old neighborhood which is still owned by a member of the original family is that of Charley Emmons, brother of my best childhood friend, Betty.

Now little remains of the buildings on the Ambuel homestead. For the most part the surrounding countryside is left to grazing cattle, and to the original homesteaders - the prairie dog, the coyote, the cactus and the sagebrush...

Aunt Louise

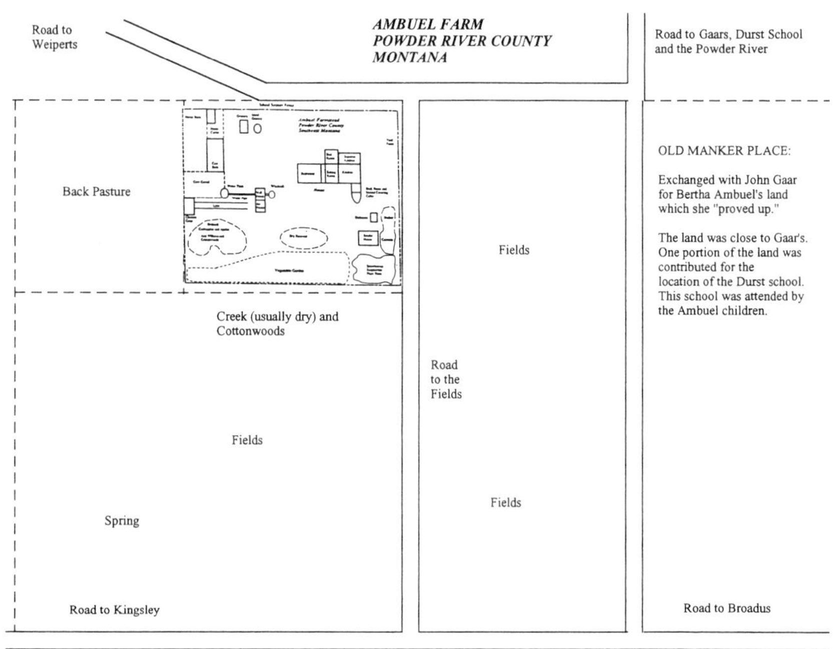
AMBUEL FARM
POWDER RIVER COUNTY
MONTANA
Road to Weiperts
Road to Gaars, Durst School and the Powder River
Back Pasture
Fields
OLD MANKER PLACE:
Exchanged with John Gaar for Bertha Ambuel's land which she "proved up."
The land was close to Gaar's. One portion of the land was contributed for the location of the Durst school. This school was attended by the Ambuel children.
Creek (usually dry) and Cottonwoods
Road to the Fields
Fields
Fields
Spring
Road to Kingsley
Road to Broadus

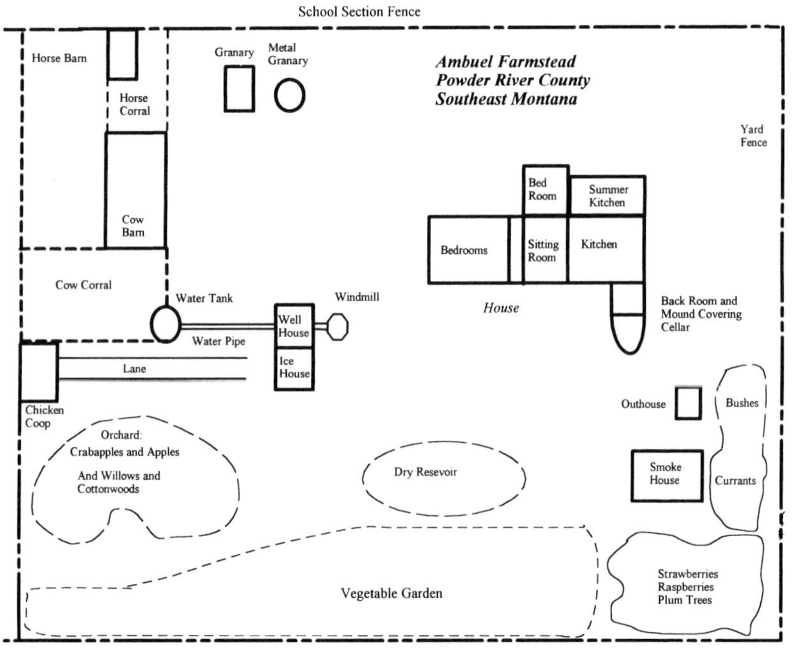
School Section Fence
Horse Barn
Horse Corral
Granary
Metal Granary
Ambuel Farmstead
Powder River County
Southeast Montana
Yard Fence
Cow Barn
Bed Room
Summer Kitchen
Bedrooms
Sitting Room
Kitchen
Cow Corral
Water Tank
Windmill
Well House
House
Back Room and Mound Covering Cellar
Water Pipe
Lane
Ice House
Chicken Coop
Outhouse
Bushes
Orchard:
Crabapples and Apples
And Willows and Cottonwoods
Dry Resevoir
Smoke House
Currants
Vegetable Garden
Strawberries
Raspberries
Plum Trees

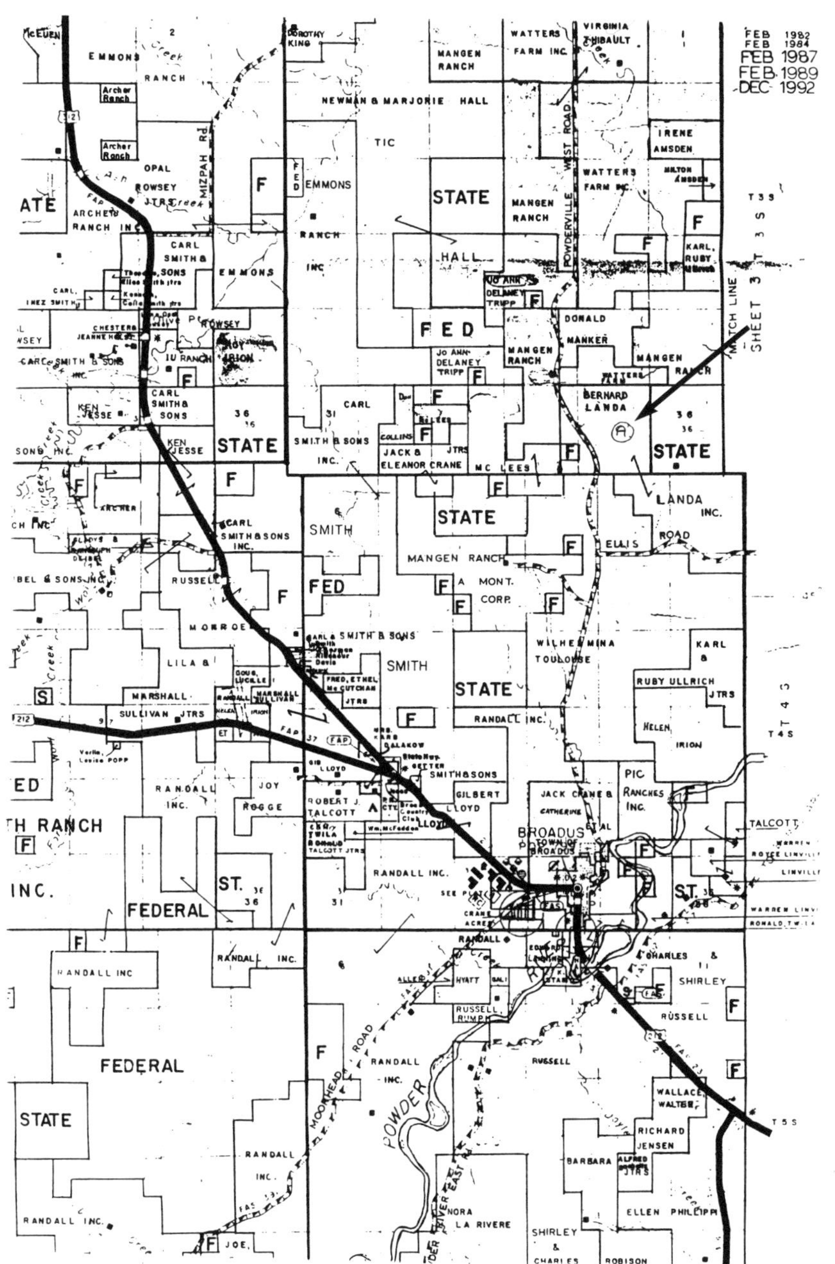

Plat Map, Part of Powder River County.
(A) marks old Ambuel place.

Letters Via Chinook

To My Grandchildren
Laura, Brian, David, Philip

CHILDHOOD MEMORIES: Teaching By Action

The old saying - actions speak louder than words - can be illustrated by these examples from my childhood. In a general way they say we do not talk about sex organs or sexual activities.

This episode happened when I was perhaps five or six years old. The younger members of the family were taking their regular Saturday night baths in the kitchen end of the kitchen-dining room, a multipurpose room with a large galvanized tub serving as a bathtub.

I asked my mother what these little balls were. (I had apparently just discovered my testes). There was no verbal answer - just a slap on my hand - actually more of a pat than a slap. One which said "we don't talk about that". There was in fact very little talk about sexual matters. We might go to the outhouse together, but we did not talk about it.

I remember one other episode from my childhood years that suggests that this may have been more than a family pattern. This involved several boys in their early school years. We were playing in the open country away from homes. Several boys used the open fields as a place to urinate. Two of them left the group apparently feeling that this was inappropriate behavior but with a variety of taunts following them: "Sissies! Ya, ya, they go home to piss in their mother's lap".

The depth of the feelings about sexual taboos is illustrated by the story of a grandmother who was asked by her daughter to get a chest xray since several of her close relatives had recently developed tuberculosis. She objected, and when pressed to get the chest xray said she was sure these tests would reveal the fact that she had in her teen years engaged in masturbation and that this secret would be revealed to everyone by the test and then everybody would know about her shameful behavior and this would be a great disgrace to the entire family.

The very deep concern about sexual activity and the methods used to impress it on at least one Lutheran member of the community probably led to an unusual sensitivity to sexual taboos.

That is all for now...Until next time

Best wishes

Be good

Keep the peace

Grandpa

Letters Via Chinook

Letters to my Grandchildren
Laura, Brian, David, Philip

CHILDHOOD MEMORIES: My Father

My father was a farm boy who grew up in Southern Illinois. His family migrated from Switzerland and was part of a German community with very little emphasis on education so that like most of his peers his formal education ended early; following the third grade he stayed at home to help with the farm work.

He was able to read and write with a somewhat limited reading vocabulary and I am sure he felt his lack of education was a distinct disadvantage; but as I listened to him talk to neighbors and relatives he was quite capable of holding his own in those discussions and it seemed to me he was better than most of them when it came to the logical evaluation of the issues.

Dad was quite supportive when his children were interested in getting more educational experiences even though I'm sure he would have welcomed their help in providing the hard work necessary to run the farm. He arranged for Louise and me to get organ lessons. To do this he purchased a pump organ which stood in our living room for a number of years. This also required the purchase of a set of mail order lessons, study guides, and the use of a metronome to help us in our practice sessions. As a result I learned a wee bit about music.

Dad was a product of the farm community but he supported my desire to go to college. This in spite of the fact that I know he would have been glad to have me stay and help him on the farm.

It seemed to me that Dad had developed a very similar set of values for himself to live by as those developed by my mother but was less inclined to attribute this to any set of religious beliefs. He did not talk about a belief in God, Heaven or Hell, or in an afterlife.

Some anecdotes about my father may help to fill in the shades of his personality. I have already mentioned the story of his strong disagreement with the Reverend Duncan described in the letter on religious education. The Reverend, at the end of his Sunday sermon, had said it was his opinion that playing baseball on Sunday was against God's will; Dad strongly disagreed with this. He did not think it was in the Reverend's role to decide what was the will of God.

Dad purchased a one third ownership in a threshing machine with two neighbors. When the owners (A,B,C) agreed to do a threshing job for owner B a serious disagreement developed about the method of calulating the charge and how it should be paid - to the point of near blows at one point in the argument.

One faction took the position that there should be no charge to a co-owner of the machine. After all, why should you pay yourself for using your own machine? The other faction took the view that this would not be fair to those co-owners with the smallest amount of threshing to be done. This was my father's position in the argument. I can remember that I was at the time sympathetic to his viewpoint but I did not say this to my Dad.

Eventually this led to the breakup of the co-ownership and I am not familiar with the details of the final agreement. I can remember him saying over and over again. "Your way is fine for the big guy, but it is not fair for the little guy". This was one of his common complaints - that too often the little guy gets gypped.

My later evaluation of the threshing machine argument led me to the correct answer which my Dad had recognized from the start. The correct way to look at this problem is to remember that each of the three owners (A,B,C) actually owned only one third of the machine, not the total ownership. In the extreme case the big guy might have 1000 hours of threshing vs the little guy one hour of threshing. When the threshing machine, like the one hoss shay, broke down all owners would be expected to share equally in the expense.

One day I was playing a pretend football game in our small front yard. I was the passer, the receiver, the kicker, the punt returner, the running back, the quarterback, etc. At first there were no observers. Then I saw Dad returning from the Manker house a quarter of a mile away. I stopped my game; I was embarrassed at being caught in such a foolish pretend game. I did not feel it was an appropriate game for a "big boy" to be playing. When Dad reached the front yard he said "Why did you stop playing your game when you saw me coming? That makes it look like you are afraid of me."

In fact I was afraid of my Dad. I'm not sure why. I do not remember ever being spanked by my Dad but I was aware that he had spanked my siblings. There was a story of an incident that was said to have occurred when I was about two years old - the terrible twos. I was obviously too young to remember it, but this is the story as told to me. My mother was trying to feed me. I was alternately screaming for something, and then refusing it when it was offered. Finally my mother gave up and said "I guess you will have to take over; I can't do anything more with him." At this point Dad jumped from his chair accidentally turning over the high chair I was sitting in and spilling my glass of milk. This action thoroughly frightened me and may well have been the trifle that led to my fear of him.

Growing up in Montana was hard in a way and I was painfully shy as a teenager. My isolation during my transition years may have contributed to that. But it was a good life with good parents and enough challenge to toughen me up for the years ahead.

That is all for now....Until next time

Best wishes

Be good

Keep the peace

Grandpa

Letters
Via Chinook

To My Grandchildren
Laura, Brian, David, Philip

Detour with Aunt Louise: Community Anecdotes and Other Tidbits

The Privy and the Tam

Community picnics and get togethers were common in our neighborhood. On this particular occasion we were visiting at the home of one of our more distant neighbors. My best friend, Betty, had come with us - she frequently "stayed over" at my home as I did at hers.

During the course of the day Betty had occasion to take a trip down the "path" to visit "Mrs. Jones". Why I was not with her I am not sure, since often these trips were community affairs. Time went by; more time went by. Eventually we noticed that she was staying an unusually long time, so a messenger was sent to investigate. The messenger discovered that she was gazing down the hole, perhaps hoping that the magnetism of her gaze would raise her tam'o'shanter from the depths.

P.S. This is the only time I am aware of a possession of value being rescued from such a humiliating fate.

P.P.S. This is a true story.

The Skunk and the Young Entrepreneurs

There was a story which circulated during my childhood days about a Broadus citizen with a problem: a skunk had taken up residence under his house.

What to do?? As anyone familiar with skunks knows, this is a most delicate situation. Some young boys came along and assured the householder that they could get the skunk out from under the house without mishap - for a fee. I think the fee was five dollars which was pretty good money in those days.

Since Mr. X was over a barrel so to speak (or more properly over a skunk), he agreed. The boys made good on their word and before one could say "Mephitis mephitis" the skunk was out from under the house and the boys had their hands out ready for their wages. Because it had seemed such a simple accomplishment and taken so little time Mr. X felt that the agreed-upon remuneration was much too steep. This indeed was akin to highway robbery.

Whereupon the boys replaced the skunk under the house; it is my understanding that the agreement was reinstated.

P.S. I cannot vouch for the truth of this story. It may be apocryphal, but given the ways of humans, varmints and boys, I think it quite possible that it is true.

Spelling

The teacher asked Johnny to spell "frog". He rose dutifully from his desk and began "fr--" "fr--" "fr--".

Karl, sitting behind him, pricked him with a pin, whereupon Johnny said "Oh gee".

Teacher said "That's right Johnny!"

P.S. This is probably NOT true, but was one of my father's favorite jokes.

Aunt Louise

Letters Via Chinook

To My Grandchildren
Laura, Brian, David, Philip

Detour with Aunt Louise and Grandpa: Politics and Sources of Information In Powder River County

Our community was not exactly apolitical, but on the other hand was not, I think, very politically involved or savvy. Perhaps I hold this view because as a child and youth politics was probably the farthest from my mind, and I paid little attention to what my elders may have said or thought about such things. In fact it was more than a decade after leaving Montana before I became interested or to any degree knowledgeable about political issues.

One of the few things I do remember was going to Broadus on election day, mostly I think because the polls were always heavy with cigar smoke. My Dad smoked a pipe, so the smell of stale cigars was unfamiliar and not to my liking. Pipe smoke on the other hand I liked; I also liked to watch my father puff away on his Granger Rough Cut, and, to please us kids, sometimes to blow smoke rings.

Probably the closest "political unit" to us was whatever entity oversaw the school. Certain lands were set aside as school sections; evidently the state provided for this and to some degree exercised oversight. There were state and county school superintendents, and exams at the end of seventh and eighth grade were administered by the state: in seventh grade Geography and Hygiene, in eighth grade the other subjects.

Through the grades we all went to country schools - the Kingsley school in the very early days, and after your grandfather and I were old enough to attend, the Durst school. Except for times when we were taught by our mother (during periods of bad weather or illness, and the last three years I was in grade school when my mother taught me at home) we attended. regularly. The Kingsley school was close enough for the kids to walk; however since the Durst school was three miles away we always rode there on horseback.

There may well have been a local school board, though I do not remember being aware of one. No doubt either a school board, or if there was none the parents of children in the vicinity - those who would attend - chose the teacher, and exercised whatever direct oversight was necessary. Teachers were always women, in many schools older women who themselves had come, usually from "the East", to homestead. Later there were younger teachers. As the girls in the wider community (from Miles City, Broadus, Coalwood, and other small towns) finished high school, some immediately became teachers. Others attended "Normal School" for a year or two and received a diploma or were in some way certified, no doubt by a state board or perhaps by the normal school itself. During the school term the teacher boarded, often with the family who lived closest to the schoolhouse. The Durst school, like most schools in southeastern Montana, was a one room school with only one teacher. Most girls remained teachers until they married. Some, as did our aunt Valesca, and a few other veterans continued teaching after marriage. A friend tells me that the school board which served in her community would not hire a married woman as teacher: with a husband to support her, why should she need to teach?

I have no idea how the teachers were paid. Since I recall no discussion of how to pay the teacher, I suppose this responsibility was assumed by the state or local government. I doubt that teachers were paid "in kind" as some preachers used to be. Salary wise I seem to recall that when my older sisters began to teach (Madeline probably in 1926, Margaret about four years later) they received something like sixty dollars a month; the going wage for hired hands was a dollar a day, so two dollars a day would have been a pretty good salary.

Montana became a state in 1889, and the earliest county divisions were quite large. By the time our parents homesteaded, Custer County had been subdivided to form two counties, Custer and

Powder River, with Broadus becoming the County Seat of Powder River County.

I recall very few of the city or county officials, although certain names stand out in my memory as being among those elected to public office or if not that, the movers and shakers of the town. From my earliest memories I recall some of those names: Heidel (banker); Holt (owner of the Reliable drug store); Straiton (who provided ambulance service to Miles City, ninety miles away and was an insurance agent); Bates (owner of the lumber yard); Blenkner and later Burton (who ran the general store); Jones (editor of the newspaper); Waite (a local rancher); Allee and later Onstad (lawyers); Miller (who indeed ran the mill); McCurdy (county clerk and recorder); Cook (barber) a role later filled by Chiesa; Turley (who ran a rooming house); Macy (who had a movie theater in Macy's hall, had his own orchestra and played for dances); and doctors James, Halleck and Amick - in that chronological order. Who ran the hotel? I do not know, but I am told the only phone in town was there.

I do not recall very "hot" electioneering, nor do I recall any burning issues during the years I was growing up. There must of course have been many issues and decisions, particularly since this was (relatively) an infant county and an infant county seat.

During my 'teens, the names of at least three elected officials were well known to me: Edith Boyes who for years was County Superintendent of Schools; Mrs. Miller, chairperson of the Broadus schoolboard (whose home also served as the local hospital, and a home away from home for high schoolers such as your Grandpa and me when we had to batch in town); Claude Anderson, who for many years was the Sheriff of Powder River County. Of more interest to me than his official position was the fact that Claude was the brother of Jess Anderson who married our sister Madeline. Madeline met Jess when she taught at Ashland, close to his ranch home on Three Mile Creek. Claude and Jess were sons of "Kid" Anderson, an early settler and cattle rancher in southeastern Montana.

Local information (and gossip) traveled to some extent by word of mouth. Since Broadus was the county seat and the largest town it was also the hub of activities for the whole county. Broadus shopping trips and celebrations (such as the Fourth of July) served to provide for contacts among members of the far flung community. A weekly newspaper, the Powder River County Examiner, was established and is still being published today. In my day the editor was Ashton Jones. Today the newspaper is edited by Joe Stuver.

There were some rural mail routes but none in our immediate community, so we had to travel eight miles to the Broadus post office to pick up the mail and the newspaper. For us this was usually a weekly expedition, at least after we had wheels, and was the opportunity also to shop for groceries and any other necessities available in Broadus. In early days mail was delivered by horseback between some of the towns. As a young girl Madeline, corresponding with a friend, wrote a letter which never reached its destination. Some forty years later this long lost letter was found (I believe at Boyes) in an old saddle bag - apparently overlooked on the last trip before the modern world overtook the frontier. So much for the pony express!

There were no telephones in rural areas so the only means of communication were by foot, horseback, lumber wagon, or sleigh during the earliest years, then by automobile as cars became more common. About once a year after we acquired a car our model T Ford made the ninety mile trip to Miles City to stock up on things not available in Broadus. Sometimes our father made this trip alone; sometimes he was accompanied by our mother. Occasionally as the youngest I was lucky enough to be included. I recall on one such trip we were returning after dark. About ten or fifteen miles from home we topped a small rise and there reflected in our headlights were perhaps fifty glowing orbs - a flock of sheep bedded down in the roadway. Not to worry. At my father's speed of twenty five miles an hour there was no danger of running into them.

The Examiner provided us primarily with local information: events in Broadus and chatty columns written by contributors from the various small towns (often little more than post offices) in the region: Boyes, Epsie, Powderville, Olive, Coalwood, Ekalaka, Ashland, Biddle, Sonnette, Stacy, Bayhorse, Moorhead, Ranch Creek, Ridge, Volborg.

As I recall, little if any state, national, and international news was carried by the Examiner, and no one I know of had news magazines or other sources of news about the wider world. The Saturday Evening Post provided glimpses of cosmopolitan life beyond Montana.

The first time I remember hearing a radio was at the home of our aunt and uncle - Valesca and Johnny Gaar. I was probably about six or seven at the time. Madeline, Margaret, and Francis' cousin Harold Fox sent us our first radio - one that he had made. Your grandpa remembers it didn't work too well. At some point we did get a working radio and it of course provided us with news of the outside world. In this case again, however, I paid little attention to such mundane matters as affairs of state. Much more to my liking were "Myrt and Marge", "Death Valley Days", and the other programs which provided entertainment, especially in the evenings.

I recall little if any discussion of state or international politics. State issues seemed rather remote and apparently were not considered to affect us much. Since this was the period between the first and second world wars, there were no burning issues involving us at an international level. The name of Senator Burton Wheeler became familiar and there was considerable interest in national politics, particularly during the depression. I remember some fairly heated discussions regarding depression era concerns. Henry Wallace was Secretary of Agriculture, and his programs of slaughtering stock during the worst drought years (in the early '30s) had a direct impact on farmers who owned cattle or sheep. I am told that the government paid twenty dollars per head for the cattle which were destroyed - and apparently none of the meat was salvaged for human use. Herbert Hoover was not loved and as I remember he was credited by many with inventing the depression single handedly. Most people I knew tended to vote for Democratic candidates. There were of course exceptions; my perception, perhaps erroneous, was that the more affluent, often the business men or elected officials living in town were more likely to be Republican.

The only wider issue I can recall being discussed in our home was on the occasion when some "outsiders" held some sort of a mass meeting in the community. Apparently our parents attended and my impression is that the visitors were explaining or perhaps extolling Communism. Evidently the crowd was hostile; my Mother seemed to think the audience was unreasonable in that they refused even to hear the speakers out. Many times after that my mother would say, "What <u>is</u> Communism anyway?" I think she never got a satisfactory answer.

The adults in our community were probably more alert to and interested in, political matters than I am aware of. It is my impression that most people took seriously the responsibility of voting. More than anything else perhaps my lack of knowledge stems from my childish disregard for this adult concern. Our parents, while teaching us to be in most ways responsible, self reliant adults, and expecting us to pull our weight as we were able, at one and the same time very much allowed us to be children unencumbered by adult worries.

Aunt Louise

Letters Via Chinook

To My Grandchildren
Laura, Brian, David, Philip

CHILDHOOD MEMORIES: The Rooster's Crow

My Dad and I were standing by the wood pile in the front yard. This was where small, relatively short pieces of wood were stacked waiting their turn to make the final dash to the cook stove.

The day was bright and cheerful. We had four roosters and the roosters were competing for top billing. Their crowing was clear and insistent.

I said, "There, that one should be a good one for our Sunday dinner. He is plump and sassy." Dad suddenly put on his "Doubting Thomas" mask. "How can you know? A crow is a crow." "Oh, but they are all different. They sound very much the same, but when you carefully listen to them they are each different. If you could record them on a graph I am sure you would find each crow is different, just like a fingerprint."

I pointed out the one I was talking about, and we captured the rooster. But I don't think I ever convinced Dad.

That is all for now...Until next time

Best wishes

Be good

Keep the peace

Grandpa

Letters Via Chinook

To My Grandchildren
Laura, Brian, David, Philip

Detour To A Recent Episode In Wisconsin: The Day I Got Lost In My Own Back Yard:

It was a bright, sunny, but slightly cool day in April. Since we had not had much sun this spring it seemed like a good day to get out and explore the bushes and flowers before spring changed into summer. I carefully stumbled down the porch steps, along the flower bed by our garage, and walked to the lot line that we share with the Wilhelm's. I found the metal post that marked the spot where our lot met the two adjoining lots. I had been there many times and it was very familiar to me. After walking in circles several times, looking at bushes and fallen tree limbs, even clipping a few, I suddenly realized that I did not recognize the back sides of any of the houses I was looking at. Except for my own I am not familiar with any of the back doors or garages.

After spending several minutes walking in circles trying to figure out where I was I saw a small group of people shooting baskets in a yard close by.

The group consisted of a four or five year old, an elderly man, and a young man. I talked to the young man and told him about my problem. He gave me his name and I recognized him as a boy who had grown up in our neighborhood, but no longer lives here. I gave him my name and address and he quickly showed me where to go. There was no problem in recognizing the front of our houses.

This was a rather scary experience. Maybe it was because I have Parkinson's Disease or maybe it was a reaction to some of the medication I take for treatment of my Parkinson's, or maybe I should stay out of back yards!

That is all for now....Until next time

Best wishes

Be good

Keep the peace

Grandpa

Letters
Via Chinook

To My Grandchildren
Laura, Brian, David, Philip

From Grandpa in collaboration with Aunt Louise: Thoughts on Philosophy, Ethics, Religion - I

It is 3 a.m. I am sitting at the kitchen table in my home in Brookfield, Wisconsin, far removed from the sod house I grew up in. I have just torn up and rewritten for the umpteenth time my words of wisdom on the complex topic of "philosophy, ethics, and religion". (I have lumped these together because I am a lumper). Previous letters have introduced you to some ideas in this area; however we have only started the task of understanding the issues involved. You should develop your own ideas, but remember to respect others and their ideas. The questions presented in the next couple of letters will cover only a few of the issues that could be included.

I do not pretend to have the answers to many of the questions that you and others ask in this area of thought; I do, however, think it is a good idea to consider them, to wonder what the answers should be and to strive to come to reasonable answers.

Before we get into the discussion of more specific items I would like to make a few suggestions. Keep in mind that many people living in different cultures have thought about and developed certain philosophical and religious answers to cope with these questions. Children begin to ask religious and ethical questions long before they grow up, and often "drive their parents nuts" with the persistence of their probing inquiries.

People in different cultures, today and in previous generations, have differing experiences, use other languages and may come to different conclusions; but at the same time there is considerable similarity from one age and culture to the next. Some ideas may seem strange to us, but we should be tolerant of the ideas expressed by others. We have much to learn from them. It is difficult to understand points of view of people who do not have a language similar to ours but I suggest that you be tolerant of differing viewpoints. Do not assume that yours is the only correct one. The history of our species suggests that all too often we have not recognized that others may be just as correct and that there may be more than one correct answer.

This is one earth and we have to live on it. Because of the rapid change in the speed and ease of transportation and the marked increase in our ability to communicate with people in all corners of the world it is more important than ever before for us to be tolerant of the views of other people in order to avoid conflict with them, especially conflict over religious views and opinions.

We should remember that the human species now has the capacity (the technology as well as the power) to destroy the earth with the atom bomb, germ warfare, toxins, and pollution or at least make it uninhabitable for our species. One of the main features of religions and society mores is the preservation of the species; but the way to promote species preservation in the modern world is probably much different than it was in the past. If we do not learn this soon we may indeed become an endangered species.

It is our tendency to be too sure about the rightness of our viewpoint so that we end up in foolish and time consuming discussion much like theologians of the past who spent hours arguing about how many angels could dance on the head of a pin. Our egotism and desire to be first lead us into foolish conflicts and silly arguments which in turn lead to war and torture. It is more important than ever to avoid or solve such foolish arguments so we can go on to the questions that really matter.

Before we start discussing specific topics, let me list a few examples. Some questions might be:

What is the nature of man?

Is there a God?

If there is no god, how did the complicated, complex world and the vast universe with its blanket of stars get built? Who made the very complex body and mind that man and in fact many animals have?

What is space? What comes after space? If space ends, what comes next? If space does not end, how does it go on forever?

What is my purpose in living?

These are just a few of the questions that might be discussed. We will not answer all these questions but at least we can begin thinking about them.

A few words about how this section on philosophy, ethics and religion will be presented: Some of the questions or ideas will be presented as discussion between our "pretend" friends - Joe and others - and will sound something like this: Sally asked "What is a miscarriage?" Joe answered "That is when the baby is born before it can live by itself." Occasionally a viewpoint or question may be presented by the moderator. In this case the message will be IN THIS TYPE and no name will be used.

Philosophical and Religious Musings: The Nature of Man; Self Sacrifice; Preservation of the Species

Is the human species good or bad or both? Is man selfish or caring, cooperative or self centered? Is he that way by nature (by heredity) or made that way because of the environment - the kind of home and community he grows up in? Is a person by nature only out to get the most he can for himself?

Is he inherently concerned primarily with his own success or does he have an inborn concern for the welfare of others including the welfare of his group and his species? How does this apply to you and me? What can we conclude by applying logic to this question?

Logic of the Survival of the Species

Survival of humans with their protracted adolescence, requiring care for a long time, does not allow for heredity to be involved only with the selfish "me alone".

Let us begin by noting that for you to be here today, that is to be born and grow up to be an adult, we know that your mother and father had to be born and live to the age when they could produce a child - you. The same is true for your grandparents and great grandparents and great great grandparents. So too it must be with all members of the human species with their long adolescent stage when they must rely on the care and protection of others.

In some species the need for a species preserving system may be provided by such a simple mechanism as the production of a very large number of eggs so that perhaps one out of a million will make it to the next generation. Therefore in contrast to humans and other mammals, fish and some other species seem to survive by overproduction of eggs.

It is obvious that for humans one must make the success rate much larger than this in order for the species to maintain itself and provide for its preservation. Otherwise we would quickly become endangered.

Maintenance of a nurturing environment for our young is necessary so that they can live long enough to produce the next generation. There must be something in our biological makeup that enables us to ensure that our children live to adulthood. When one looks for examples of species preserving mechanisms one must look at the element of self sacrifice.

To explore further some of the questions about motivation we will look more closely at the nature of man/woman and the evidences of self sacrifice and concern for others we find in relationships. The following examples are from my experience on our homestead farm.

Mother's Protection of Newborn: Maternal Sacrifice; Mother Love

Examples of self sacrifice for the good of others is seen most prominently in the willingness of mothers to risk their own life and limb to protect their young. I have seen a mother mouse carry four infant mice, one at a time, away from the threat of danger (me) as she moved her young to a place she deemed safer.

Have you ever seen a group of medium sized birds, swallows for example, dive bomb a larger bird such as a crow or hawk which is threatening the nest of the smaller birds? On some occasions the swallow may actually strike the head of a human who is threatening its nest by getting too close to it.

Even the domestic chicken (hen at least) will strive to get into the protective action. When a hawk gets too close to the tree tops of the feeding yard, the group of feeding chickens will flutter along the ground as if they are about to take off in flight even though they have lost their ability to fly more than ten to twenty feet.

I have noticed the behavior of horses when a group of them are in the pasture together that suggests a herd instinct to protect the young. When a group of them, say ten to fifteen, are joined by a colt they all seem to crowd around the colt as if to protect him. Among our group of horses was a distinctly smaller one, almost as small as a Shetland pony. This small horse, now a full grown adult, was right in the middle of the protecting herd.

Self sacrifice and concern for others must be one of the mechanisms which has allowed our species as well as others to survive. However today's environment is vastly different from the past and the survival of the human species perhaps requires a new and different mindset. To return to an earlier thought: we now have the ability to destroy the world or make it uninhabitable. We have the capacity to make ourselves an endangered species.

The argument is not whether heredity or environment is involved in the nature of man; it appears to be both. Our ability to show self sacrifice and our willingness to fight for our species, our country, our nation, our religion, our ideas, our clan or our gang are further evidences of the phenomena we are discussing and seem to work through both pathways. We need to think about these and other important questions instead of wasting our time on foolish arguments. In looking for answers we might note the nearly universal tendency of religions to build something into their teachings that give people a goal in life beyond their own selfish self interest. We also need to learn to control our egotism; if we believe in God, we cannot assume that we and we alone have a pipeline to his knowledge and wisdom.

That is all for now....Until next time
Best wishes
Be good
Keep the peace

Grandpa

Letters Via Chinook

To My Grandchildren
Laura, Brian, David, Philip

Thoughts on Philosophy, Ethics, Religion - II

The last letter provided some general thoughts on the lumped topic of Philosophy, Ethics and Religion. This letter will examine ideas that are more limited and specific.

Sally asked "What is a miscarriage?" Joe said, "That is when the baby is born before it can live on its own." Jill added, "To stay alive the baby must rely on its mother's womb, lungs, blood flow...." Betty chimed in "What about all this new fangled stuff I keep hearing about such as artificial insemination and organ transplants?" Joe grumbled "Yes, that is going to foul up everything. Nobody will know who is who or what is what. Oh, I guess we will stumble through somehow. We may not be smart, but we are lucky." Betty said "Yes, like with the atom bomb. Do you suppose that the big bang was triggered by some psychotic crack-poisoned fool?"

Sally was still curious. "Does the baby die first and then the miscarriage come? Or does the miscarriage cause the death of the baby?" Don said "It really doesn't make much difference; the end result is the same." Betty objected, "But the baby is a person when the egg is fertilized."

HOW DO YOU KNOW? CAN YOU TALK TO HIM? CAN HE TALK TO YOU? CAN YOU UNDERSTAND HIM? HOW DO YOU KNOW IT'S A HUMAN? ONE CELL, FERTILIZED OR NOT, DOES NOT LOOK MUCH LIKE A HIM OR A HER. I WONDER HOW LONG THIS ARGUMENT WILL GO ON. IT REMINDS ME OF THE STORY OF HOW THE RELIGIOUS LEADERS OF THE PAST WOULD SPEND HOURS ARGUING ABOUT HOW MANY ANGELS COULD DANCE ON THE POINT OF A NEEDLE. MAY I MAKE A SUGGESTION? NEXT TIME LET'S TAKE ON A SIMPLE QUESTION LIKE 'WHO IS GOD'.

Joe said to me: How come you don't believe in God?

I NEVER SAID THAT I DON'T BELIEVE IN GOD

Oh, so you are one of those angry guys!
THE WORD IS 'AGNOSTIC', JOE

Angry, swamby, you are just trying to show off.
WHO IS GOD?

God is the unknown, the all powerful creator of the world.

OF THE UNIVERSE?

Yes, and of space and non-space.

DOES SPACE STOP OR DOES IT GO ON FOREVER?

How can anything go on forever?

HOW CAN IT STOP AND THEN HAVE NOTHING BEYOND THAT POINT?

THAT IS WHY I AM AN AGNOSTIC. I DO NOT KNOW THE ANSWER TO SOME OF THESE QUESTIONS.

So, said Joe, I suppose that when you are being chased by a tiger and the tiger is gaining on you you won't pray to God for help since you don't know if there is a God. Oh, he's a chicken! He might pray to God even if he says he doesn't believe in Him.

YOU ARE RIGHT! IN THAT SITUATION I PROBABLY WOULD PRAY TO GOD. BUT THAT DOES NOT PROVE THAT GOD EXISTS. MY REACTION WOULD BE EMOTIONAL, NOT RATIONAL OR LOGICAL.

But if God saved you, wouldn't care.

BUT HOW CAN YOU MAKE YOURSELF BELIEVE IN GOD IF YOU REALLY DON'T?

That is all for now......Until next time

Best wishes

Be good

Keep the peace

Grandpa

Letters Via Chinook

To My Grandchildren

Laura, Brian, David, Philip

CHILDHOOD MEMORIES: From the Homestead to the Degree of Doctor of Medicine

It seems an unlikely happening. Can a boy born into a poor family living through the depression on a Montana homestead, a family which has only one person (a nurse) in a health related field, earn an M.D. degree? It happened, aided and abetted by a number of lucky breaks and fortunate circumstances.

In retrospect I have tried to identify some of the events and factors that enabled me to earn the Doctor of Medicine degree from the University of Chicago in 1946. A key factor was my parents who were supportive of their childrens' desire for education even though the family was barely able to maintain the economic viability of the small homestead. They supported my interest in school and learning, approved my desire to get more education and helped me in any way they could to stay in school.

My father who had been removed from school at the end of the third grade to help with work on the family farm in Illinois came from a farm culture which put little importance on education. Dad broke with this culture and encouraged me to go to college when the time came. He believed that every child who wanted it, and showed some success, should have the opportunity to get an education.

A significant number of my mother's family, who were immigrants from Norway, had advanced educationally, particularly as teachers and ministers. My mother herself became a teacher as did the two sisters who joined her as Montana homesteaders.

I am sure that the support of my parents was a major factor in stimulating my interest in science, education, and learning in general. This also encouraged me to get the kind of grades that prepared me to go on to advanced educational programs.

In addition to the long history of educational activities of my mother's family, both in Norway and the United States, the Preus family in Norway set up a loan fund to provide for the advanced education of family members. The rules of the legacy required that in this country the recipient must go out of state for higher education. In Europe the requirement was to go to another country. I received a loan from this fund which enabled me to attend Luther College in Decorah, Iowa where I received a bachelor's degree in pre-medical studies. This loan was crucial, since it permitted me to obtain a college degree from a highly competitive pre-med program.

At about this time I read *Microbe Hunters*, a very interesting book by Paul de Kruif. This was also a great influence on my decision to become a doctor. At this time I was much interested in science, but reading this book changed my major area of interest from the stars to the world as revealed in the microscope.

Good grades in high school (I was valedictorian of my class) and college which I finished cum laude, as well as a good score on the medical aptitude test, were additional elements making medical training possible.

After teaching in the biology department at Luther for a year following graduation, I had enough money saved to pay for the first quarter of medical school. The V-12 naval reserve program paid the remainder of my tuition as well as provided me with money for living expenses. My graduation from Luther College and my acceptance into medical school made it possible for me to begin the medical program at the University of Chicago, but I would not have been able to become a doctor without the help of the loan from Norway and the V-12 program.

That is all for now...Until next time
Best wishes
Be good
Keep the peace

Grandpa

Letters
Via Chinook

To my Grandchildren
Laura, Brian, David, Philip

CHILDHOOD MEMORIES: Our Faithful Pony, Chip

Chip was our faithful pony who carried Louise and me to our one room country school on many a school day. He finally graduated from eighth grade in the same year as my graduation from elementary school.

From our home to the country school was only three miles (an easy walk for country children) but we learned early to conserve energy for the really important things in life - like games. We usually had Chip thoroughly loaded for the trip to school. That meant that I occupied the saddle and Louise straddled his back behind the saddle.

The school was located on a large area of open prairie. Since we could not turn our pony loose we put a halter on him and tied the other end to a small log. This meant he could pull the log around so as to reach grass to eat but still not wander too far away. When school was out it was easy to find and bridle him for the trip home.

If teamed up with another horse, Chip was expert at hanging back and letting his mate pull most of the load; and when we would leave school one would think he was barely able to move. However when we got close to home he would suddenly perk up.

That is all for now...Until next time
Best wishes
Be good
Keep the peace

Grandpa

P.S. (from Aunt Louise)

I remember one time when your grandpa had forgotten to tighten the cinch. As we started home and went down the ravine crossing the school yard everything was fine; but when we started up the other side - whoops! - I slid off over Chip's tail. I don't believe faithful Chip blinked an eye, and I was none the worse for the experience.

Letters Via Chinook

To my Grandchildren
Laura, Brian, David, Philip

From Grandpa in Collaboration with Aunt Louise
CHILDHOOD MEMORIES: The Natural Beauty of Eastern Montana

Most of these Letters Via Chinook have focused on experiences that relate to home, family, school and community. However over the years I have spent a lot of time in solitary activities. Some of these have been individual projects but I have also taken time to contemplate and appreciate the beauty of Eastern Montana - an appreciation which has made me aware of almost spiritual feelings associated with the awesome aspects of the natural world. This is especially true when the prairie is viewed at dawn and dusk.

One of my individual projects consisted of planting flowers along garden pathways and scattered among the vegetable plots. For years I planted morning glories and moon flowers in front of our "summer kitchen", and was rewarded by a display of colorful flowers.

It took me two years to construct a flower box outside our kitchen window - the window where our swing was located. This flower box was constructed of rocks picked up from our fields and pastures and hauled from there to the site, carried in my arms or in a small wagon. Mostly the rocks were just stacked like a yard fence but I used a little cement to help fortify the box at key spots.

For a couple of years I struggled to build a tennis court in a portion of the yard which had not yet yielded to the plow. I thought this would be possible since we already had some expertise in using a fairly flat portion of the pasture for our baseball diamond. Since I often played the shortstop position on a baseball team I was quite aware of the uneven nature of the surface of such an infield. Instead of bouncing into your glove the baseball was quite likely to bounce erratically above your glove and strike you in the chest or face. In spite of my best efforts with a hoe and rake I was never able to get a smooth surface on my tennis court.

As I matured into my adolescent years I began to appreciate the unique beauty of Eastern Montana. We do not have in Eastern Montana the spectacular mountain ranges, the forests, the caverns and canyons, the trout streams, the waterfalls and the top of the food chain wild life, grizzlies for example, seen in the western part of the state.

I remember thinking how come? Then I said to myself, "When God came to Western Montana he had a lot of vim, vigor and materials. Well God ran out of vim, vigor and materials when He got to the prairies of Eastern Montana - all the spectacular items were used up." All that was left were pine hills, grasslands, willows and cottonwoods. But the beauty of Eastern Montana has a distinct quality all its own. I would rather sit on the top of Cradle Butte than climb the highest peak of the Rocky Mountains.

The subtle beauty of the Eastern Montana landscape is subdued and diffuse, but in its own way is as mighty as the grandeur of Western Montana. As dawn gives way to the blazing summer sun and bulging thunderheads form in the afternoon sky, as heat lightning flickers to the west, and at nightfall as dusk fades to dark and the black sky becomes a blanket of stars traversed by the milky way what more profound spiritual feelings could one experience anywhere?

That is all for now...Until next time
Best wishes
Be good
Keep the peace

Grandpa

Letters Via Chinook

To My Grandchildren
Laura, Brian, David, Philip

CHILDHOOD MEMORIES: Native Americans

During my childhood years in Montana I never had contact with Native Americans. In retrospect this seems strange since our home was close to the center of what had been the Plains Indians' territory. It was about seventy five miles from the site of Custer's last stand at the battle of the Little Big Horn. That battle and other military action between the U.S. army and the Indian tribes - the ongoing Indian wars - eventually led to the destruction of the Plains Indians' culture and way of life. Large numbers of Indians were removed from the wide open spaces to less desirable territories or to reservations.

The Indians never had a system of private land ownership in the way the homesteaders did. The tribes did of course claim some territoriality among themselves over hunting rights; but they did not own "mother earth" nor could they sell her. Since hunting of buffalo was the main source of their livelihood the Plains Indians of course did not welcome intruders such as the homesteaders who threatened their food supply.

I never heard any serious expressions of prejudice for any of our neighbors. This may have been related to the fact that there were no Black Americans, no Jews, no Japanese, no Chinese, no Mexicans ... no Indians ... in the community. The people who had homesteaded or bought land in the area all seemed to be from Europe or from the eastern or midwestern United States.

I do remember one incident when my Dad, who had been to Broadus for supplies, commented that a Jewish man had been in Broadus looking for a place to set up some kind of a shop. The man was advised by a group of business men that that would not be a good idea. Dad was noncommittal.

Some years later I remember overhearing a discussion by my older sisters and some other relatives and neighbors. Referring to a certain colored person someone said: "He acted like he was just as good as we are". So one did find a certain amount of prejudice.

There was of course occasional talk about Indians. The term "Native American" came along many years later. In general Indians were looked on as savages. This was perhaps related to the U.S. army and the Indian battles. Also, the Indians were considered to be heathen: they did not believe in God or Jesus. It was the Christian's duty to save them. Unlike the Eskimos there was no recognition of their social structure or their religion. Only in recent years has there been an effort to really understand and appreciate Indian society.

That is all for now...Until next time
Best wishes
Be good
Keep the peace

Grandpa

Letters Via Chinook

To My Grandchildren
Laura, Brian, David, Philip

Detour with Aunt Louise: Self Sufficiency on the Montana Prairies

I have heard it said that the veneer of civilization is extremely thin. When that veneer is scratched, as is true of furniture, or the rind of fruit, deterioration is often not far behind. I think this is particularly true of modern civilization. Can you imagine what would happen - what does happen in regions of war and catastrophe - when this veneer is destroyed, when the systems of sustenance (food and water supplies, medical materials and facilities, not to mention the complex commercial network integrated with those systems....) break down?

Pioneering and homesteading were characterized by a mimimum of supporting systems, so that the individual or family unit was largely responsible for its own welfare. As a biology instructor I sometimes likened the progression of society to the progression of species from the single celled, (one cell carries on all life functions) through the colonial organism (where there is some specialization and division of labor) to the complex multicellular organism (with cells losing their totipotency and becoming highly integrated and interdependent). Pioneering life was (and sometimes still is for those daring souls who venture into the hinterlands far from "civilization") close to the situation of the single celled protozoan. Homesteaders more nearly resembled the colonial protozoan; and the modern city dweller, to a lesser degree his fast disappearing rural counterpart, is like the multicellular organism.

Recalling what has gone before in these Letters, it is no doubt obvious that self sufficiency played an enormously important role in life on the Montana prairies. I believe my experiences on a Montana farm have enabled me to be more self sufficient than some - though certainly my life would be severely strained if deprived of the support systems I am used to today, and I am not sure that I could survive on a homestead. On the other hand my penchant to save all sorts of apparently useless things (string, bottles, cans, buttons, Christmas wrapping....) and a certain degree of ability to make necessity the mother of invention has no doubt been influenced by the experiences of my youth. Perhaps the immense importance of the community that existed on the prairie has likewise been the inspiration for my strong need for and gravitation to community in my adult life.

You have already been introduced to a number of instances of the self sufficiency which reached into all areas of life on the prairies in the '20's and '30's. The land was a gift of the government, awarded under the Homestead Act of 1862 with ownership passing to the homesteader after building and living on the property for a prescribed number of years. The rest was up to the homesteader. One or two of the buildings on my Dad's homestead (later enlarged by a small, contiguous parcel, bought or traded) may have been moved from another location. However most of the buildings were built by my father with whatever help was available. The outbuildings were all made of log with the exception of the sod smokehouse; the house was built of log and sod. Only one structure - a steel granary - was commercially made, and that late in the generation our family spent on the farm.

Furniture and other household equipment was mostly bought. Our kitchen range burned wood and coal. It was equipped with a warming oven and a reservoir which provided a ready supply of warm water. We had a heating stove in the sod sitting room/bedroom; and a small "laundry" stove which heated the children's bedrooms at night. Chairs, tables, the occasional dresser, and the wardrobe in my parents' bedroom were all bought as were the beds - with the exception of the trundle bed which was hidden away under my parents' bed during the day. The little ones graduated from this when they were old enough and bed space in the bedroom became available with the departure of the older siblings as they left for high school. Dishes, pots and pans, buckets, boiler and galvanized tubs were all bought, as was the washing machine, acquired probably about the time I completed grade school. Churns, the cream separator which stood in the kitchen, and the pump organ, which my father brought home while I was still in grade school, were also purchased. Trundle bed, woodbox, bookcase, wall "closets", shelves, stands of various sorts, and some cupboards, were all home made. Also home made was a large storage box for outdoor wraps which doubled as a kitchen window seat and another similar one providing extra storage in my parents' bedroom.

Outdoor equipment with the exception of a home made stone boat and a small sleigh was virtually all bought: water tank, farm machinery, large sleigh, harnesses for the work horses, saddles and bridles for the saddle horses. I think the shallow original well may have been dug by my Dad and some of the locals; however the deeper well completed when I was perhaps eight years old was done by a professional well driller.

Our home was never equipped with running water, electricity, gas, refrigeration, indoor plumbing or phone. The only "running" water was what was run by foot from well to house, garden, or flower bed or carried by pipe from the stock tank to the closest garden plots. The reservoir on the kitchen range, and the water pail with its single dipper kept the job of carrying water to a daily or twice daily excursion except on washdays and Saturday nights. Because Eastern Montana is fairly windy the windmill kept the wellhouse tank and the stock tank full summer and winter. One was not extravagant with water: kids took baths once a week in a galvanized wash tub, a ritual replaced by "spit baths" (sponge baths) as we grew older. There were no bath tubs of the modern variety. Daily ablutions such as they were were dependent on wash basins. I seem to have no recollection of how my parents bathed; I'm sure they could not fit into the wash tubs we kids used, but perhaps the tub accommodated their feet and the procedure was a kind of modified spit bath. I do not recall that we ever rigged up any kind of "shower" such as I have seen in some primitive environments.

Since plumbing did not exist, toilet necessities were provided by the "two-holer" behind the house, forty paces from the front door. This was a perfect place to which to repair when it was your turn to dry the dishes. No one dared intrude on this sanctum sanctorum. In case of illness and sometimes to avoid a nocturnal excursion (especially in inclement weather) the slop jar, also known more elegantly as the chamber pot, served its purpose.

House and water were heated by wood and coal. Wood was cut on our "forty" along the river, probably part of Mom's homestead. It was brought home and sawed into chunks, then split into stove-sized pieces which were stacked in a huge woodpile in the yard, dwindling through the year until it could be replenished during the summer months. Early on, coal was mined by the family from veins in the pine hills. Later we had coal delivered and I am still trying to remember where it was stored - perhaps in the cellar, perhaps in an outdoor coal shed.

Before the purchase of our washing machine, washing was an all day process. The old (as I remember, it was always old!) copper boiler was put on the kitchen range to boil the bejabers out of the white clothes. From there the steaming whites and later the coloreds were transferred to the line of tubs set on benches beside the kitchen table. This is where the youngest family member, standing on the edge of the boiler and reaching for after-dinner leftovers slipped into the boiling, soapy water and carried the effects for many a day. The first tub held the washboard and soap where the final stages of washing were completed. Then came two tubs of rinse water. Following their trip through the hand wringer the clothes were hung outdoors on the clothes line, summer and winter. After their exposure to sun, wind, freezing temperatures or whatever the season provided they came in smelling lovely and fresh - a fragrance not to be matched by my modern electric dryer. The eventual purchase of a gas washing machine made the task of weekly washing much easier than the old boiler and washboard routine.

Cooking was done on the kitchen range; no hurrying things along with gas or electricity. Sometimes this actually simplified tasks: if the oatmeal or wheatmeal was put on the stove in a double boiler after supper, by morning it would be tranformed into a nice warm, steamy breakfast to nourish and please the entire family - that is if you liked oatmeal or wheatmeal! Usually our cereal was wheatmeal, made by grinding our own wheat; once our Mother even concocted "grape nuts" out of ground wheat and molasses and who knows what else.

Ironing of clothes was done with sad irons. I never knew why they were so called - perhaps because it was a sad task to use them. Actually I rather liked to iron. They were heavy, real "iron" irons with detachable handles. Two or three were put to use at once, one to go about the business of ironing, one or two reserves-in-waiting, heating up on the top of the kitchen range.

Sewing was done on a treadle sewing machine, ours a Singer with a head that could be lowered into the bowels of the machine, so when the cover was closed the stand doubled as a table or work surface. All the girls learned to sew, taught by our Mother and, in my case at least, encouraged by the opportunity to compete in the fall fair by making aprons and other simple articles. On one occasion Margaret, apparently distracted, ran the sewing machine needle through her finger. I am sure this did not require a visit to the doctor (if indeed there was a doctor in Broadus at that time) but was probably treated by Mom - possibly by soaking it in kerosene which seemed to be a universal treatment in our household.

Kerosene lamps provided household light. Your grandpa decorated these lamps by floating colored tissue paper in the kerosene which filled the bowl. With their glass pedestals and chimneys they provided a homey atmosphere for family conversation and late night reading - sometimes disturbed by the mortal thrashings of a moth which, lured by the siren flame, ventured too close to the chimney top. In later years a Coleman gasoline lamp brightened our home, though it replaced our kerosene lamps only occasionally. The gasoline was contained in a metal tank; this had to be pumped up to maintain pressure and the light was provided by mantels which on first use were transformed from little cloth bags into filmy, almost ash-like gossamers. I still remember the ceremony of the first lighting, but my fascination continued even after the novelty had worn off. We rarely if ever used candles, except to decorate our Christmas tree.

Outdoor light was provided sometimes by flashlight, but more often by kerosene lantern. Particularly in the fall and winter, and even on summer days when the men worked late in the fields, evening chores had to be completed in the dark. There was something friendly about the sight of a lantern light bobbing along as Dad and the boys moved from house to barn and back again.

Since we had no refrigeration we depended on the cellar to store butter, cream, milk and eggs as well as autumn vegetables. In the summer we supplemented cellar storage by keeping milk, home made root beer, watermelons and other things in a shallow portion of our well-house water tank. Butchering was done only after temperatures were below freezing, so that the carcasses could be left hanging long enough to allow for the necessary work of preparing the meat for smoking and canning.

We never preserved foods by drying or freezing, but we did keep vegetables in the cellar throughout the winter: potatoes, onions, and squash in bins, carrots and other root vegetables buried in sand. Some things we preserved by pickling or fermenting - pigs' feet, cucumbers, sauerkraut; some foods such as beefsteak were fried and put down in lard. Pork fat was rendered into lard and along with butter used as our shortening. Some of the meat Dad peddled from door to door in Broadus, for the princely sum of ten cents a pound.

Whole milk was separated morning and night, with the skim milk kept for home use including the needs of the animals. Cream, besides what was reserved for table use and baking, was stored in cream cans in the cellar and periodically taken to Broadus for sale. Since to my knowledge there was no creamery in Broadus, the cream was probably shipped to Miles City. We churned our own butter, first with a crockery churn (equipped with a sort of paddle which was raised and lowered to turn the cream into butter), later with a barrel churn. This gave us a plentiful supply of buttermilk to drink and to use in baking. Butter, like cream, eggs and meat, was sometimes sold for the few cents of cash it would provide. We did not store ice, so while we kids doted on ice cream we rarely made it at home. Occasionally, if we had a heavy hailstorm we would collect enough ice to make a freezer full, and we brought the makings to community events where others provided ice for the freezing.

Milk was our main beverage, but we also sometimes drank postum and cocoa which of course we had to buy; the coffee grinder on the wall provided the wherewithal for the grownups' cup of "Java" while the kids at least could enjoy the aroma of the freshly ground coffee beans.

With no phone, and initially no car, communication was by foot, horseback, lumber or spring wagon, and sleigh. After the family acquired a Model T Ford the status of travel and communications improved considerably, though one still thought twice before taking to the road. One did have to buy gas after all, and, while we were not paupers we were cerainly not affluent.

We bought white flour and sugar by the hundred pounds. The sacks provided dish towels and material for other purposes. Graham flour we ground from our own wheat, and cracked wheat was served up as wheatmeal for our morning cereal. Bread and cinnamon rolls were generally made fresh each Saturday, and Saturday nights usually found the "five little Ambuel's" at the kitchen table dunking hot cinnamon rolls into cold milk. Besides bread we baked the usual - biscuits, cakes, cookies, doughnuts, pies, and, mainly at Christmas, Norwegian delicacies from our Mother's heritage.

Our garden and orchard produced most of the vegetables and fruits known to man (at least Americans): radishes, lettuce, tomatoes, cucumbers, cabbage, onions, peas, beans, kohlrabi, spinach, swiss chard, corn, beets, squash, raspberries, strawberries, currants (black and red), compass cherries, muskmelon, watermelon, apples (red and yellow crabs and winesaps). In the glossy seed catalogs of today one can seldom find some of the more exotic fruits, such as ground cherries and husk tomatoes, which grew in our garden. Nature added to our store through the wild fruits we picked in season: chokecherries for sauce, syrup and jelly; wild plums for sauce; and rarely the tiny, orange-red buffalo berries which yielded delicious jelly.

From these fruits of garden, field and ravine almost everything that could be was preserved for use during the winter. The hardy vegetables and fruits were stored fresh as long as possible. Some were put down in brine or pickled in vinegar, cabbage was transformed into sauerkraut. Peas, beans, corn, tomatoes, beets, crab apples, husk tomatoes, chokecherries and wild plums were canned, as were fruit juices to be made later into jellies and jams.

I cannot recall our buying any vegetables, but we did occasionally buy oranges, more frequently lemons for lemon pie and summer lemonade, and in the fall peaches for eating and canning, and concord grapes for juice and jam. We bought brown sugar, honey in large, square, ten gallon cans, and sometimes tins of syrup and molasses. Only rarely did we have "store bought" bread.

Our protein was plentifully supplied, not only by the milk our small herd gave us, but also by the meat from the steers and pigs butchered each fall. Milk was used for drinking, in puddings, creamed vegetable dishes, and made into cottage cheese - the only cheese I recall having. Occasionally we had wild fowl such as sage hens, prairie chickens, and grouse. Since there were virtually no game animals in our area, and neither Dad nor the boys were hunters we never had wild game as was possible in Western Montana. Dad prepared head cheese and pickled pigs' feet from the pigs we butchered; he also smoked bacon and hams in our sod smoke house. Chicken, both fresh and canned was always available, and we had plenty of eggs except at times when the hens were brooding. We had virtually no seafood, except canned cove oysters and sardines and no lamb or mutton. My Mother's background was Norwegian and we almost always managed to buy some lutefisk for our Christmas celebration. There must have been a sizable population of Scandinavians in Miles City since this delicacy was usually available at that time of year. To my mind my Mother's greatest culinary skill was in her meats. At butchering time we had fresh steaks, both beef and pork. However fresh meat was not available very long, so her canned pork loin, beefsteak, beef stew, and meat balls saw us through most of the year. We never made fancy sausage such as my father's family made in Southern Illinois, but we always had meat balls - ground from beef with our sturdy metal grinder.

Some clothing was locally available, but more often purchased from the "wish book" - the "Monkey Ward" and Sears Roebuck catalogs: shoes, sized by standing on a paper while the outline of the foot was traced; bib overalls; coats and some other outer wear; sweaters; possibly a suit for men and older boys, occasional dresses for women and girls; hats and caps (mostly bill caps for the boys); "long handled" underwear. This kind of underwear was a case unto itself. The leg had to be wrapped around and held in place while one rolled up one's coarse stockings over the "long handle" leaving an unsightly bulge above the ankle. By the time we came along shoes were generally laced, rarely buttoned, and since zippers had not arrived - at least in Montana - overshoes were fastened by buckles.

Other clothing, mostly dresses and aprons for the girls and women, was sewed at home by our Mother and sometimes by our Aunt Valesca. I still remember with delight the dark green silk dress Aunt Valesca made for me. I think it was made out of "second hand" material - it had been someone else's dress before. The entire front of the bodice was tucked. The back was unmatched, but not visible since it was covered by a jacket. I loved the color and the tucking. Sometimes Mom even sewed boys' coats and jackets, one of which someone swiped the first time your Grandpa wore it to high school.

I do not remember anyone doing any hand knitting at home. However Dad had a knitting machine with which he knit stockings. I remember them as shapeless tubes with no heel and a straight, and uncomfortable, seam across the toe. Stockings for the kids and I guess for the men were held up by garters, for women by corsets or garter belts equipped with fasteners. If I remember, silk stockings arrived on the scene, in Montana at least, about the time Madeline (fourteen years my senior) finished high school and began teaching.

We also received a lot of hand-me-down clothing passed from child to child as well as from older cousins. The barrels of clothes received from our mother's sister, Rosine Moen who lived in Mason City, Iowa were particularly appreciated. The arrival of those barrels was "Christmas in the summer time".

Empty sugar sacks made wonderful dishtowels; flour sacks and burlap sacks could be used as material for clothing and other things. Gunny sacks were too coarse to be desirable for purposes other than rough storage. Ticking was sewn to form pillows which were stuffed with feathers and mattresses filled with corn husks or with straw from our threshings - not goose down, but adequate, with a friendly crackle when one moved in bed! Sheets, curtains, portieres and other such necessities were often home made.

"Planned obsolescence" was not part of our vocabulary, and things that were damaged or wearing out were repaired and repaired again. Knives which needed sharpening found their way to the big grindstone in the yard, where Dad sharpened and Mother poured cooling water over the stone. Dad also soldered our pots and pans by means of a soldering iron heated with a blow torch. I loved to hear the hiss of the blow torch and to watch the long rope of solder make a silvery puddle as the red hot soldering iron melted it into the hole to be mended.

When our shoes wore thin or developed holes, Dad was able to half sole them. With a good grip on his hammer and a metal "foot" over which to fit the shoe he did a good and sturdy job. Not only could he give two footed creatures soles - he was able to shoe our horses.

Dad had at one time been a barber and we kids got the full benefit of that. Whenever we got too shaggy it was time to pin a towel around our shoulders and submit to his barber shears. The clippers, always dull, took the final bits of shag from the back of our necks while we cringed as they also took their "pound of flesh". Our Mother's hair was long and she wore it in a bun on top of her head, so she was not in need of haircuts, but she served as barber for our Dad. At that time men could get a haircut for a dollar, but in our less than affluent household that was one dollar too much.

At Christmas we usually cut our own tree. Only once do I remember not having a proper tree; our father's illness made it impossible to make the annual drive to the pine hills so we resorted to a scrawny little leafless plum cut from our yard. Every year popcorn and cranberries were strung on thread, and along with paper chains and other paper ornaments made our Christmas tree gay; but the final touch depended on the multicolored little candles attached by small silvery holders. Nothing could be more beautful than the tree decked out in its finery, made more fine by the flicker of the lighted candles as we sang Christmas carols, listened to the Christmas story, and opened our presents.

Christmas presents were mostly home made, though we kids sometimes received bought presents: a sled, skis, a doll, doll buggy - things that it would be difficult or impossible to make. We kids usually made glass paintings, shaving pads, gifts of woodwork and the like as our Christmas presents to the family; even the grownups shared in this home-made kind of Christmas with dresses, scrap books and such, kept carefully from the prying eyes of those for whom the gifts were designed.

While I would no doubt be lost without many of the conveniences and amenities I enjoy today, I still feel a sense of satisfaction when I can achieve some goal working against the odds, employing a degree of independence, testing my self sufficiency. For that I think I owe a debt of gratitude to my homestead upbringing. That does not mean that I do not value the interdependence that goes with being part of a true community. It seems to me that a healthy balance between independence and interdependence, between community and individuality, provides an ideal atmosphere for the development of a contented and well adjusted person. Perhaps too it is one of the basic requirements for that most elusive of states: peace, good will toward men.

Aunt Louise

Letters Via Chinook

To my Grandchildren
Laura, Brian, David, Philip

Railroad Trip

We sat quietly in the passenger car of the Great Northern cross country railroad line. The clickety clack of the train's wheels added to the monotony of the scene. As we gazed out the window of the train we were struck by the subtle changes in our view as the fence posts flashed by the open windows. Indeed the landscape was significantly altered as we viewed the scene to the North, South, East, and West.

As we gazed North with the train moving South the individual posts of the barbed wire fences would sometimes weave like drunken cowboys, or, depending on the angle of view, might flash by like the pickets of a fence. Looking East the sameness of the primary landscape was broken by small irregular pine hills and the occasional cottonwood and willow in the creek bottoms; to the West the grasslands were punctuated only by sagebrush and cactus. Viewing the monotony of the open prairie scene it was easy to be lulled into the sense of vast horizons - things yet remaining to be explored!!!

That is all for now...
Best wishes
Be good
Keep the peace

Grandpa